sf bay area 2nd ed.

eat.shop sf bay area
was researched, photographed and written
by jon hart

S0-AJR-545

about eat.shop

the first thing to know about the *eat.shop guides* is that they are the only guides dedicated to featuring locally-owned eating and shopping establishments. the guides feature a fresh mix of places from posh to funky, spendy to thrifty, old school to just-opened, hip to under-the-radar. what do these places have in common? uniqueness, innovation and passion. you know these places weren't conceived out of a marketing plan, but out of someone's single-minded drive to create something special in their city.

this *eat.shop guide* is a "plus" size edition, so instead of featuring just 90 carefully picked businesses, there are over 120 swell places. why the super-sizing? though san francisco is filled with gems, we felt this time around that we couldn't ignore what's going on in the east bay. often noted as the "brooklyn" of san francisco, there's no denying that it's a hopping area.

enough explaining, here are a couple of things to remember when using this guide:

• explore from neighborhood to neighborhood. note that almost every neighborhood that's featured has dozens of great stores and restaurants other than our favorites that have been featured in this book. you'll find a listing of the neighborhoods, their street boundaries and the businesses within them on a following page.

• make sure to double check the hours of the business before you visit by calling or visiting their website. often the businesses change their hours seasonally.

• the pictures and descriptions of each business are representational. please don't be distraught when the business no longer carries or is not serving something you saw or read about in the guide.

• at the *eat.shop guides*, the culture of a city is a major part of the experience. so whittle out some time to soak in the arts, the music, the architecture and the even the street scene.

• if you're visiting the city, we know you'll need a rest eventually. so we've listed some of our favorite hotels to help you make your choice.

• to truly experience the city san francisco-style, hop on bart (www.bart.gov) which will take you from the city to the east bay. another transportation option in the city? rent a bike, it's a great way to see the city. and of course, don't forget the world famous cable and streetcars (www.sfmta.com).

• this is the second edition of *eat.shop sf bay area* (note: the first edition was called *eat.shop san francisco*). there are more than a 100 businesses new to this edition. if you would like to see the businesses that were featured in the previous edition, they are listed on a following page. also their addresses and phone numbers can be found on the *eat.shop* website. and remember, don't get rid of your previous editions, think of them as just part of the overall "volume" of *eat.shop sf bay area*. every business that has been featured in this guide, past and present, is fantastic. if the business is no longer featured in the book, it's not because it's lost its luster, but because there are so many incredible establishments deserve to be noted. so make sure to reference the "past edition" list also, as many of the bay area's true gems are on it and are not to be missed.

jon's notes on the sf bay area

lured away from the midwest by the promise of mountains, wide open spaces and possibility, i moved to the west coast in 1993. i planted my roots in portland, but for my first summer vacation i travelled to the bay area. driving across the golden gate bridge, the first time, i caught a glimpse of a shimmering city improbably propped upon it's unlikely hilly terrain. i knew at that moment, i would have a lifelong relationship with this city. as many other tourists have done, i jumped on the cable car at powell street and held tight for the roller coaster ride of city streets. the exhiliration of that first tour has never faded, even after many visits to this wonderful city.

as years have passed i have returned for a dose of big city verve, momentous art shows at sfmoma or the yerba buena center, to share fantastic food with wonderful friends, or to find a perfect pair of shoes for a special occasion. each time the promise that seems inherent in these hills, water, bridges, and open minded people reveals itself and a wonderful time is had. i knew that day in 1994 that the city by the bay was different and special. i hope this list of remarkable businesses will lead you to discover it too.

here are some of my favorite non-eat.shop things about the sf bay area:

1> bridges of the bay area: the golden gate and the bay bridge. walk on them, drive on them, look at them, they are modern day miracles of what human beings can create.

2> wave-organ: at the eastern edge of golden gate recreation area is a work of environmental art where you can literally listen to the movement of the ocean in what sounds like the largest sea shell in the world.

3> de young museum of fine arts: located in beautiful golden gate park this is one of the most exciting pieces of architecture to be built in the united states this century. the art is not bad either.

4> the headlands: a community of artists and writers located on this absolutely gorgeous piece of land in the marin headlands. check www.headlands.org for upcoming events.

5> glide memorial church: an inner city church for literally everyone—even non-believers. the choir is so contagious, and stories so inspiring here, even the biggest cynics will end up hugging their neighbors in the pews. go to www.glide.org for times and address.

eat. shop. enjoy.

jon hart
jon@eatshopguides.com

the master list

san francisco

the richmond
eat: aziza
roadside bbq
shanghai dumpling king
shop: kamei kitchen supply
parklife

pacific / presidio heights
shop: birch
erica tanov
nest

marina
eat: lucca delicatessen

russian hill / polk gulch
eat: 1550 hyde
biondivino
bob's donuts
cheese plus
swan oyster depot
the candy store
shop: cris

chinatown
shop: the wok shop

north beach / telegraph hill
eat: liguria bakery
nua
shop: al's attire
alla prima
aria
double punch
mixed use
goorin hat shop
yone of san francisco

jackson square
eat: bocadillos
coi
shop: area
eden & eden

embarcadero / soma
eat: boulette's larder
shop: fantastico

tendernob / union square
eat: bar crudo
canteen
sam's grill

shop: in fiore
salon des parfums
tsurukichi indigo

tenderloin
eat: bourbon and branch
farmer brown
saigon sandwiches

hayes valley
eat: essencia
miette confiserie
true sake
shop: alabaster
fiddlesticks
mac
nida
peace industry
propeller
rose and radish

potrero hill / dogpatch/ bayview
eat: piccino
shop: arch
flora grubb
the ribbonerie

the mission
eat: bar tartine
bi-rite creamery & bakeshop
dosa
la taqueria
mission pie
pizzeria delfina
range
ritual coffee
spork
tartine bakery
the blue plate
the front porch
weirdfish
walzwerk
shop: 826 valencia
candystore
creativity explored

house of hengst
minnie wilde
monument
paxton gate
self edge
stem
x21
zoë bikini

noe valley
eat: chocolate covered
lovejoy's tea room
shop: church street apothecary
nisa san francisco

castro / market street
eat: zuni
shop: my trick pony
the seventh heart

japantown / western addition
eat: on the bridge
shop: harputs market

upper and lower haight / nopa (no. of the panhandle) / cole valley
eat: nopa
the alembic
shop: cookin'
doe
egg & the urban mercantile
gamescape

glen park
eat: gialina

outer sunset
eat: underdog
shop: mollusk surf shop

east bay

old oakland
eat: tamarindo
shop: drift

rockridge
shop: twenty two shoes
august

temescal
eat: bakesale betty
pizzaiolo
shop: article pract

piedmont
eat: césar

gourmet ghetto
eat: guerila cafe
shop: herringbone

elmwood
eat: ici
shop: slash
tail of the yak

4th street
eat: sketch
vik's chaat corner
shop: cactus jungle

west berkeley
eat: seasalt
shop: magnet

monterey market
shop: supple

misc. berkeley
eat: crixa cakes
sophia cafe
tokyo fish
shop: addison endpapers
hida tool

previous edition businesses

san francisco

the richmond
eat: pizzetta 211
thanh thanh café
shop: tal-y-tara tea & polo
shoppe

pacific / presidio heights
eat: cafe lo cubano
chouquet's
florio
sociale
shop: beau
flicka
march
pumpkin

marina
eat: a16
shop: atys
wingard

russian hill / polk gulch
eat: dynastea
shop: la place du soleil
la tulipe noire
velvet da vinci

chinatown / north beach / telegraph hill
eat: stella pasticceria e caffé
shop: delilah crown

jackson square
eat: frisson
shop: thomas e. cara, ltd.
william stout books

embarcadero / soma
eat: miette pâtisserie
shop: sfmoma museum store

financial district / downtown
eat: canteen
tadich grill
yank sing

hayes valley
eat: blue bottle coffee co.
citizen cake
hotel biron
the orbit room
shop: bell'occhio
dish
friend
gimme shoes
lavish
stitch

potrero hill / dogpatch/ bayview
shop: dandelion

the mission / outer mission / bernal heights
eat: bombay ice creamery
country station sushi
emmy's spaghetti shack
mi lindo yucatan
paplote
st. francis fountain
zante pizza & indian cuisine
shop: dema
virginia howell's

noe valley
eat: 24th st. cheese company
shop: the ark
the french tulip
wink sf

castro
eat: lime
shop: nancy boy

upper and lower haight / nopa (no. of the panhandle) / cole valley
eat: rnm
rosamunde sausage grill

you can find the addresses and phone numbers for all of these businesses at: eatshopguides.com

if businesses that were featured in a previous edition are not on this list, it means they have closed.

also note that the previous edition of this guide only featured san francisco (no east bay) businesses.

neighborhood boundaries : map info

sf

the richmond district
north of fulton to presidio, from masonic west to the pacific ocean

pacific / presidio heights
north of bush to broadway, from van ness west to masonic

marina
broadway north to sf bay, van vess west to the presidio

russian hill/polk gulch
from california north to lombard, leavenworth west to van ness

chinatown
california to the south, kearny to the east, mason to the west, columbus to the north

north beach / telegraph hill
mason to the west, columbus to the southwest, broadway to the south, the bay to the north

jackson square
sansome west to kearney, washington north to broadway

embarcadero/soma
market from 12th to the sf bay south to king

tendernob/union square
montgomery west to van ness, geary north to california

tenderloin
mcallister and market north to geary, powell west to van ness

hayes valley
fell north to fulton, franklin west to wesbter

potrero hill/dogpatch/bayview
jerrold north to 15th, sf bay west to potrero

the mission
from north of mission and cesar chavez to 12th, potrero west to dolores

noe valley
30th north to 20th, dolores west to diamond

castro / market street
market to the south from castro street to van ness, north border hickory from van ness to webster, waller from webster to castro

japantown/ western addition
north of fulton to bush. from van ness west to masonic

upper and lower haight/ nopa (north of panhandle)/ cole valley
parnassus north to fell, fillmore west to golden gate park

glen park
san jose and bosworth to the south and east, 30th to the north, glen canyon to the west

outer sunset
kirkham north to golden gate park, sunset boulevard west to the pacific ocean

east bay : oakland

old oakland
south of 11th to nimitz fwy, from broadway west to mlk

rockridge
east of telegraph to the oakland hills, south of berkeley city limits to the intersection of 51st street and broadway

temescal
centered on telegraph, between broadway and shattuck to the east and west, from claremont south to macarthur

piedmont
centered on piedmont between broadway and pleasant valley

east bay : berkeley / albany

gourmet ghetto
(aka upper shattuck)
centered on shattuck from vine street south to university

elmwood
centered on college, from stuart south to woolsey

4th street
centered on 4th from cedar south to university

west berkeley
san pablo west to the sf bay, university south to dwight

monterey market
centered at hopkins near sacramento

directions

the boundaries noted to the left are what border the neighborhood from north to south, east to west.

a couple of things to know about san francisco, streets run from east to west and avenues run from north to south. numbered streets are in the mission and downtown usually and in the richmond and sunset neighborhoods, streets are alphabetical.

if you want to get to the east bay, take the bay bridge by car or bart by train. if you want to go to marin county or the wine country, head over the golden gate bridge.

maps

because we wanted to give you the most detailed maps possible, our city maps are now available on line. please go to:

http://maps.eatshopguides.com/ sf_ed2/

here you will find a map of the entire city, with indicators showing where each business is. bookmark this url into your pda, and you'll have the mapping data right with you as you explore.

if you don't own a pda, but want a great street map of the city, the *eat.shop* authors love the *streetwise* maps. they are indispensable tools when you need a take-along map with lots of detail.

where to lay your weary head

there are many great places to stay in the bay area, but here are a couple of my picks:

hotel palomar
12 4th street / 415.348.1111
hotelpalomar-sf.com
from $379.00
restaurant: the fifth floor
notes: luxurious boutique hotel near union square

hyatt regency san francisco
5 embarcadero center / 415.788.1234
sanfranciscoregency.hyatt.com
from $239
bar: 13 views bar
notes: classic modernist hotel made famous in "high anxiety"

the orchard garden hotel
466 bush street / 415.399.9807
theorchardgardenhotel.com
from $300
restaurant: roots
notes: brand new 'green hotel'

hotel tomo
1800 sutter street / 415.921.4000
jdvhotels.com/tomo
from $109
notes: fun and funky, inspired by japanese pop-culture

waterfront plaza hotel (in oakland)
10 washington street / 510.836.3800
waterfrontplaza.com
from $199
notes: views of the bay, some rooms with fireplaces

a couple of other options:
the clift (clifthotel.com), the huntington hotel (huntingtonhotel.com),
hotel metropolis (personalityhotels.com) and hotel des arts (sfhoteldesarts.com)

jon's twenty favorite things

01 > italian combo on super sour at lucca delicatessen

02 > salted caramel ice cream at bi-rite creamery

03 > carnitas taco at la taqueria

04 > meatball and red onion pizza at pizzaiolo

05 > flan de coco at tamarindo

06 > black cod with braised fennel and preserved lemon at boulette's larder

07 > masala dosa at vik's chaat shop

08 > spiced churros with hot chocolate at nua

09 > raisin focaccia at liguria bakery

10 > roasted root vegetable couscous with housemade harissa at aziza

11 > handmade glass top boxes from addison endpapers

12 > jean shop wallet at august

13 > dries van noten embroidered shirts at mac

14 > ron gilad void table at propeller

15 > cast iron woks at the wok shop

16 > deep oudh perfume at salon des parfums

17 > indigo died t's at tsurukichi indigo

18 > surprise balls at tail of the yak

19 > ton fisk finnish ceramics at eden & eden

20 > copper rain chains from hida tool

1550 hyde café & wine bar

neighborhood wine bistro

1550 hyde street. corner of pacific
415.775.1550 www.1550hyde.com
tue - thu 6 - 10p fri - sat 6 - 10:30p sun 5:30 - 9:30p

opened in 2003. owners: kent liggett and pete erickson chef: pete erickson
$$: all major credit cards accepted
dinner. wine. reservations recommended

sf : russian hill > **e01**

in san francisco, amazing wine flows like water over niagra falls. so finding a great wine bar should be as easy as finding a trashy tv show on the e! network. *au contraire mon frère.* with this much to choose from, one must narrow the focus. at *1550 hyde,* the cozy and inviting space, candlelit and convivial, calms and prepares you for the treats that await. the succulent grilled chicken is marinated in yogurt which gives it an inexplicable razzmatazz and the pot de creme is as rich and thick as donald trump. along with a fab wine list, *1550 hyde* is *une bonne trouvaille.*

---

imbibe / devour:
frédéric magnien côtes de nuits-villages
morey coffinet bourgogne
farro salad with porcini, cacciature salami & favas
kona kampachi crudo with cucumber & coriander
yogurt-marinated hoffman gamebirds
potato gnnocchi with morel mushrooms
scharffen berger chocolate pot de creme
sformato di caprica (goat cheese custard)

11

aziza

modern moroccan cuisine
5800 geary boulevard. corner of 22nd
415.752.2222 www.aziza-sf.com
wed - mon 5:30 - 10:30p

opened in 2001. owner / chef: mourad lahlou
$$ - $$$: visa. mc
dinner. full bar. reservations recommended

sf : richmond > **e02**

my meal at *aziza* could only have been better had i instantly grown another stomach. chef/owner mourad lahlou graciously sat with me as dazzling dishes of modern moroccan plates arrived. seemingly simple roasted vegetables and couscous with housemade harissa was astounding and i quickly devoured it. as dishes continued to appear, my sampling slowed. by the time the strawberry and candied rose petal parfait arrived, i raised the white flag and sadly only took pictures. the downside to this job is lack of capacity, but don't feel too bad for me—someone has to do it.

imbibe / devour:
kumquat cocktail with sicilian tangerine cognac
rhubarb & vanilla bean cocktail
baked giant lima beans
full belly farm roasted beets
roasted root vegetable couscous with harissa
hoffman ranch guinea hen
devils gulch ranch rabbit with hungarian paprika
strawberry & candied rose petal parfait

bakesale betty

comfort bakery

5098 telegraph avenue. corner of 51st
510.985.1213 www.bakesalebetty.com
tue - sat 7a - 7p

opened in 2002. owner: michael camp   owner / chef: alison barakat
$: all major credit cards accepted
breakfast. lunch. coffee/tea. first come, first served

east bay : oakland : temescal >

bakesale betty's buttermilk fried-chicken sandwiches are more than just a habit; they are an addiction. there are throngs of east bay folk dependent on them. i lined up one day to experience this seductive food that has made so many lose their will power. one bite of the succulently spicy, deep-fried chicken breast on a heavenly hoagie bun smothered in crisp and tangy coleslaw turned me into a full-fledged junkie. there's more than one vice here: the cookies and cakes are also addiction-worthy. my name is jon and i love *bakesale betty* (hello, jon).

imbibe / devour:
clover orange juice
mclaughlin royal coffee
buttermilk fried chicken sandwich
rhubarb orange scone
betty's chicken pot pie
lemon bars
betty's sticky date pudding
ginger cookies

15

bar crudo

modern raw bar

603 bush street. corner of stockton
415.956.0396 www.barcrudo.com
mon - thu 6 - 10:30p fri - sat 6p - 11p

opened in 2005. owner: tim selvera. owner / chef: mike selvera
$$: all major credit cards accepted
dinner. reservations recommended

sf : nob hill > **e04**

that purr you hear? the deep rumbling sound of satisfaction? that's me when i think about the healthy, bright and satisfying meal i had here. this cuisine really speaks to my inner kitty. *bar crudo* is a raw bar, which is a sort of half-sushi, half-tapas bar. run by the selvera brothers, tim smoothly manages the front while mike heads up the open kitchen, from which the incredible cubes of arctic char and dayboat scallops appeared, all fresh as could be and spiked with flavors like tobiko and ginger. the only thing that would make this experience more perfect would be a long catnap.

imbibe / devour:
st. bernardus, abt 12, belgian beer
domaine alain cailbourdin pouilly fume
dayboat scallops
lobster salad
marinated nova scotia mussels
arctic char cubes with horseradish, tobiko & dill
yellowfin tuna cubes with ginger, soy & sriracha
artisan cheese plate

bar tartine

warm bistro with buzz

561 valencia street. between 16th and 17th
415.487.1600 www.tartinebakery.com
lunch thu - fri noon - 2:30p brunch sat - sun 11:30a - 2:30p
dinner tue - wed, sat 6 - 10p thu - sat 6 - 11p

opened in 2005. owners: elisabeth prueitt and chad robertson chef: jason fox
$$: all major credit cards accepted
breakfast. lunch. dinner. reservations recommended

sf : the mission >

the *bar tartine* folks have the magic touch. they have one of the most esteemed bakeries around. and now they have a great bistro housed in one of the most comfortable rooms in the city. but beware—with its name discreetly printed on the window and the black exterior, it takes well tuned food-ar not to miss it. once inside the pleasant glow, the worn marble bar beckons you to enjoy the hearty food. the squid and pork belly could only be better when accompanied by *tartine's* jaw-dropping bread. to prove that magic is afoot, try the chocolate ganache cake, it's supernatural.

imbibe / devour:
cotes du luberon chateau la canorque
radio-coteau pinot noir
steelhead gravlax & beet salad with greens
local squid & pork belly with egg salad
dayboat scallops with favas, endive & salsify puree
marin sun farms marrow & grilled bread
gnocchi with sweet peas & hen of the woods
chocolate ganache cake with beet ice cream

bi-rite creamery & bakeshop

small batch artisanal ice creams, sorbets and confections

3692 18th street. corner of dolores
415.626.5600 www.biritecreamery.com
sun - tue, thu 11a - 10p fri - sat 11a - 11p

opened in 2006. owners: kris hoogerhyde, sam mogannam and anne walker
$: mc. visa
treats. first come, first served

sf : the mission > **e06**

i have come to a definitive conclusion. salted caramel ice cream is the most addictive frozen substance on earth. it was in a contest with brown butter pecan for awhile, but the answer is now clear—i crave salted caramel ice cream nine times out of ten. it's this mysterious super-substance that makes my mouth start to water whenever i'm near 18th and guerrero, the home of the new *bi-rite creamery*, brought to you by the beloved *bi-rite grocery* people across the street. don't let my compulsion sway you, though. all the flavors here are great. but did i tell you about the salted...

imbibe / devour:
lorina lemonades
extremely dark housemade hot chocolate
salted caramel ice cream
brown butter pecan ice cream
white tiger-honey lavender ice cream
  with berry compote
apple upside-down cake
chocolate soufflé cake

biondivino

italian and austrian wine boutique

1415 green street. corner of polk
415.673.2320 www.biondivino.com
mon - sat 11a - 11p sun noon - 9p

opened in 2006. owner: ceri smith
$$: all major credit cards accepted

sf : russian hill > e07

with a city newspaper that publishes a supplemental called "wine week," you know you are in a city that loves the grape. ceri, who opened *biondivino* a year ago, is passionate for wine and took a leap of faith to follow her dream. when a friend's retail space became available, she quit her job and moved cross country to open this beautiful shop dedicated to italian and austrian wines. it's a beautiful thing having a resource like ceri teaching about the esoteric charms of super tuscans and rieslings. now let's talk about the chronicle's column "earthquake roundup."

imbibe / devour:
wines:
  ronco del gnemiz
  kurni oasi degli angeli
  bruno de conciliis
  palari
  damijan
  edwardo valentini
amedi chocolates

bob's donuts

donut deliciousness

1621 polk street. between clay and sacramento
415.776.3141
24 hours a day, seven days a week

opened in 1970. owners: aya and don ahn
$: cash
treats. first come, first served

sf : russian hill > **e08**

having supposedly reached the age of reason, i know what will happen if i eat too many heavenly donuts. but, i am not so jaded that i can sluff off at my job. and my job is to seek out the gems. in order to fulfill my contract, i had to sample several varieties at *bob's donuts*. this is old school donuts and drip coffee at its best. like the donuts i often muse about, they were soft but substantial. when bitten, into produced that tell-tale uumph—paydirt. and the glaze left a happy crackle smile around the lipline—perfect. just another day at the office.

imbibe / devour:
farmers brothers coffee
hot tea
good old, raised glazed donuts
jelly-filled donuts
old-fashioned donuts
bear claws
cinnamon twists
apple fritters

bocadillos

modern tapas bar

710 montgomery street. corner of washington
415.982.2622 www.bocasf.com
mon - fri 7a - 11p sat 5 - 11p

opened in 2004. owners: gerald and cameron hirigoyen chef: robert petzold
$$: all major credit cards accepted
breakfast. lunch. dinner. first come, first served

sf : jackson square > **e09**

"small dishes" sounds anti-intuitive doesn't it? nobody ever says "let's go out for some tiny food!" well then, they have never experienced the convivial charm of spain nor been to *bocadillos* where the small dishes come with huge flavors. here the tapas tradition mostly sticks to its spanish roots with the serrano ham and calamari with romesco proudly waving spain's flavorful flag of national pride. just order some plates (i dare you to try to stop at just a few), a glass or three of wine, and i guarantee you will understand the small plate phenomenon.

imbibe / devour:
house white wine
tempranillo
sautéed pimientos de padron
lamb burger bocadillos
whole grain salad
potato & bakalao salad with aioli
baby back ribs with honey & sherry glaze
"arm of a gypsy" with hazelnut mousse

boulette's larder

exquisitely prepared locally-gathered foods
1 ferry building marketplace. southeast corner on the bay
415.399.1155 www.bouletteslarder.com
mon - fri 8a - 6p sat 8a - 2:30p sun 10a - 3p

opened in 2003. owners / chefs: amaryll schwertner and lori regis
$$: all major credit cards accepted
breakfast. lunch. dinner. dinner reservations only

sf : embarcadero > **e10**

i love eating lunch at *boulette's larder*. in its beautiful space, like the pantry from "babette's feast", one can savor the years of experience that amaryll has creating some of the best food available in this city. the simple preparations of fish and local ingredients are anything but simple once you taste the complexity of their clean flavors. and here's something really extraordinary— private dinners at *boulette's*. imagine the scene: you and your friends eating amaryll's amazing food while gazing at the sparkling bay just outside the door now this is a true san francisco treat.

imbibe / devour:
eastern european style hot chocolate
fresh-pressed martin's orchard orange juice
roasted baby beets & their greens with tahini
pulled pork shoulder sandwich
black cod with braised fennel & preserved lemon
broccoli de cicco with taleggio toast
rhubarb & strawberry shortcake
chocolate mousse cake with grand marnier

bourbon and branch

speakeasy
www.bourbonandbranch.com

opened in 2006. owners: brian sheehy, dahi donnely and doug dalton
$$: all major credit cards accepted
full bar. reservations recommended

sf : the tenderloin > e11

the other *eat.shop* authors and i are pretty competitive. each is off in his or her respective city looking for the rarest, most fantastic, secret place to include in these books. kaie was all up on her high horse one day when she found a hidden burek place in queens. to that, i counter with *bourbon and branch*. an email is required to find the password and address of this hidden prize. once you are in, you will find an incredible room befitting its prohibition-era inspiration and a spectacular selection of bourbons served to you by some of the best bartenders in s.f. take that, kaie.

imbibe:
cocktails:
  the elder flower champagne cocktail
  french 75
  blood & sand
elijah craig 18 year old single barrel bourbon
hirch 16 year old reserve bourbon
ritten house rye
talislar scotch

canteen

comfort food made with soul

817 sutter street. corner of jones
415.928.8870 www.sfcanteen.com
tue 6p - 10p wed - fri 11:30a - 2p, 6 - 10p sat 8a - 2p, 6 - 10p sun 8a - 2p

opened in 2004. owner / chef: dennis leary
$$: all major credit cards accepted
brunch. lunch. dinner. reservations recommended

sf : nob hill > **e12**

speaking in sweeping generalities (my only fluent language), it's easier to do more than less. it takes a more confident chef to make a memorable bowl of soup with minimal ingredients than it does to make one filled with endangered cuddle fish roe or truffle-infused bee pollen. chef dennis masters simplicity with ease (or so it seems). the fresh pea soup at *canteen* had the flavor of a spring morning, making you realize you are in excellent hands. this place is small and modest with just a few booths and a counter with stools, so it's intimate dining without fuss. lucky us.

imbibe / devour:
saintsbury carneros pinot noir
st. paulina beer
potage st. germain
roasted chanterelles with onion puree
steak sandwich
gravlax
rigatoni with asparagus & mushrooms
vanilla soufflé

césar

top notch tapas with excellent wine selection

oakland: 4039 piedmont avenue. between 40th and 41st
1515 shattuck avenue. between cedar and vine
510.883.0222 www.barcesar.com
mon - sun noon - midnight

opened in 1989. owners: richard mazzera, dennis lapuyade and stephen singer
chef / owner: maggie pond
$$: all major credit cards accepted
lunch. dinner. full bar. catering. first come, first served

east bay : >
oakland : piedmont / berkeley : gourmet ghetto

once upon a time, césar and panisse were famous characters from the films of marcel pagnol. nowadays the restaurants to whom they lent their names are much better known. opened next door to its fictional and real life friend, *chez panisse*, *césar* was started by three *panisse* alumni providing top notch tapas and a killer wine selection. *césar* worked so well, a second location was opened in piedmont. at both places the tapas tradition is followed with first rate dishes like salt cod and potato cazuela. add to the mix a sangria *césar* and you are sure to live happily ever after.

imbibe / devour:
buddha's passion cocktail
flor de césar
beets & boquerones
semolina flat bread with eggplant jam
baby octopus & english peas
pollo asado a la costa brava with grilled scallions
slow-cooked pork & repollo escabeche
bread pudding with orange-caramel sauce

35

cheese plus

cheese shop and gourmet grocery

2001 polk street. corner of pacific avenue
415.921.2001 www.cheeseplus.com
mon - th 10a - 7:30p fri - sat 10a - 8p sun 10a - 7p

opened in 2005. owner: ray bair
$$: mc. visa
lunch. grocery. treats. first come, first served

sf : russian hill >

cheese plus is a good name, though i'm thinking maybe it could have been called *cheese exclamation point*. ok, i understand that maybe this moniker is a bit less catchy, but the point is that, like me, owner ray is clearly a fan of what milk and a little mold can become. the selection of over three-hundred cheeses is splendidly accompanied by artisanal foodstuffs like charcuterie, wines and chocolates. the selection is so fine, i just thought of another appropriate good name: **%#@%& cheese*!!!

imbibe / devour:
chimay grand réserve
le village sparkling apple cider with cinnamon
cheeses:
  fleur vert
  persille beaujolais
  isle of mull
  boulette d'avesne
guittard chocolate

chocolate covered

exotic chocolates and cynotypes
4069 24th street. between noe and castro
415.641.8123
mon - sun 11a - 7:30p

opened in 1994. owner: jack epstein
$: all major credit cards accepted
treats

sf : noe valley > **e15**

you are in luck, readers. i have done exhaustive research for you. this research involves studying the mood altering effects of chocolate. i have eaten loads of the stuff so i can profess that chocolate does, as lesser scientists have concluded, elevate your mood. in fact, chocolate triggers the production of opioids. and here's more good news, *chocolate covered* has one of the most extensive collections of this joy-inducing stuff around. jack offers it in all flavors and with all sorts of added ingredients like plum and caramelized bacon. whoa, can you be too happy?

imbibe / devour:
chocolates:
  ginger soaked in sake
  lillie belle fleur de sel
  zotter coffee, plum, & caramelized bacon
  poppa bear's chocolate
  date & shiitake mushroom chocolate
  john kelly fudges
  señor murphy's pistachio chili nut bar

coi

modern cuisine
373 broadway street. corner of bartol
415.393.9000 www.coirestaurant.com
tue - sat 6p - 10p

opened in 2006. owner: paul einbund owner / chef: daniel patterson
$$$: all major credit cards accepted
dinner. reservations recommended

sf : north beach > e16

high end restaurants, especially in the bay area, seem to fall into two camps. one looks for incredibly fresh ingredients and makes an effort to bring out the intrinsic value of those flavors. the others start with the same premise but take the fresh ingredients to another level through combinations with other flavors or rigorous cooking techniques. *coi* is in the latter category. celebrated chef daniel peterson knows that a beet is delicious on its own but asks: wouldn't it be more interesting if it were highlighted by soy, bonito, and konbu? the answer is absolutely, yes.

imbibe / devour:
96 talisman pinot noir
foie gras & braised endive
zuckerman's asparagus with lemon sabayon
truffled ricotta pudding, peas & spring onions
slow-cooked farm egg, stewed cepes & farro
poached & seared liberty duck breast
warm vanilla cakes, strawberries & olive oil
bittersweet chocolate parfait & cucumber ice milk

crixa cakes

scratch-baked hungarian baked goods

2748 adeline street. between shattuck and stuart
510.548.0421 www.crixa.net
tue - thu 9a - 6p fri - sat 9a - 7p

opened in 1998. owners: zoltan der chef/owner: elizabeth kloian
$: all major credit cards accepted
breakfast. treats. coffee / tea. first come, first served

east bay : berkeley : berkeley bowl >

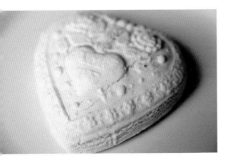

it seems all of the western world's great cuisines have their own take on baked goods. the french like to layer, taking flour and butter to delicate heights. italians are more utilitarian, using what's available to make breads and seasonal crostatas. at *crixa cakes,* there's an eastern european point of view. where confections are denser and often filled with poppy seeds or nuts and flavored with spices like cardamom and cinnamon. everything here is made from scratch, just steps away from the counter. and if you've never had a bizet with cream, step right up. it's calling your name.

imbibe / devour:
metropolitan teas
macglaughlin coffee
bizet with cream
király chocolate raspberry cream cupcake
budapest coffee cake
potato piroshki
the great flodni
pavé vergiate

dosa

south indian cuisine

995 valencia street. corner of 21st
415.642.3672 www.dosasf.com
brunch sat - sun 11:30a - 3:30p
dinner tue - thu, sun 5:30 - 10p fri 5:30 - 11p sat 5:30p - 11p

opened in 2005. owners: emily and anjan mitra chef: senthil kumar tamilnuadu
$$: all major credit cards accepted
dinner. brunch. reservations recommended

sf : the mission > **e18**

finding an excellent dosa, a southern indian, thin and crispy, golden crêpe made from lentils and rice with spicy fillings, is always a special treat. finding one made this well and served with the likes of the sinful crush cocktail makes me feel like i am starring in a music and dance number in a bollywood spectacular. one bite of the paneer dosa dipped into the fresh coconut or tomato chutney, and the music starts. my mouth is chewing, but it feels like my hips are shaking. perhaps next time i should just have one sinful crush.

imbibe / devour:
house made chai
sinful crush cocktail
dahi vada
spring dosa
paneer & romaine
onion pakora
paneer & peas uttapam
rasmalai

essencia

modern peruvian restaurant

401 gough street. corner of hayes
415.552.8485 www.essenciarestaurant.com
lunch mon - fri 11:30a - 2:30p
dinner mon - thu 5:30 - 10p fri - sat 5:30 - 11p

opened in 2007. owners: carmen and juan cespedes
owner / chef: anne gingrass-paick
$$: all major credit cards accepted
lunch. dinner. reservations recommended

sf : hayes valley > **e19**

here is a prediction: the peruvians are coming. i am speaking about restaurants because peruvian cuisine is one of the most interesting and diverse cusines in the world, on par with chinese and indian. it has influences from at least four continents mixed with its own ancient history. case in point, *essencia*. here you will find traditional peruvian foods like an octopus salad with celery hearts or the 'chicha,' a peruvian drink made from spiced purple corn and fruit juices. with delicious and unusual treats like these, i say welcome, peru.

imbibe / devour:
chincha spiced purple corn juice
sumarroca dry muscat
shrimp, scallop & mussel ceviche
cumin roast pork loin with red onion, cilantro & lime
crab & potato cakes with avocado
'triple' chicken & walnut salad sandwich
granavan mousse with fresh strawberries
'alfajores' butter cookies with caramel

farmer brown

southern food with urban cool

25 mason street. corner of market
415.409.3276 www.farmerbrownsf.com
mon - sun 5p - midnight bar 5p - 2a

opened in 2006. owner / chef: jay foster
$$: mc. visa
dinner. full bar. happy hour. reservations recommended

sf : the tenderloin > **e20**

the food world has trends just like fashion. one day shoulder pads are out of fashion and the next everyone looks like crystal carrington. lately, there has been a re-appearance of the food of the american south to which i say... yeeha! fried chicken, jambalaya, pulled pork, bring it on! this is honest cuisine, the backbone of the red, white and blue. at *farmer brown*, you get american classics prepared with a dose of urban cool. with dishes like the crispy cornmeal catfish with candied yams, this place will be in style for a long time.

imbibe / devour:
housemade ginger-beer rum punch
maple manhattan
handcut kennebac & sweet potato fries
crispy cornbread catfish with candied yams
pan-fried meatloaf
braised berkshire pork shank
chocolat beignets with strawberry sauce
strawberry rhubarb pie

49

gialina

neighborhood pizza bistro

2842 diamond street. corner of kern alley
415.239.8500 www.gialina.com
mon - thu 5 - 10p fri - sat 5 - 10:30p

opened in 2007. owner / chef: sharon ardiana
$$: all major credit cards accepted
dinner. wine / beer. first come, first served

sf : glen park > **e21**

gialina is in glen park and so yes, it's a bit of a hike but (i'm channeling homer simpson here) mmmmm, chocolate pizza. i defy you to come up with a more provocative combination of mouth-watering-but-fabulously-bad-for-you foods. ok, there's lardo and deep-fried pound cake, but *gialina* doesn't serve them and i digress. this is a bustling pizzeria with a neighborhood bistro feel with its comfortable, modern interior and vibrant clientele. the outstanding pizzas have unique combinations created with locally available ingredients. and oh my, the chocolate pizza.

imbibe / devour:
villa giada barbera d'asti
blood orange soda
pizza:
　dandelion greens, sweet italian sausage & fontina
　fennel, baby leeks, black olives & ricotta salata
　the atomica
　chocolate & mascarpone
salt cod cakes with meyer lemon aioli

guerrilla cafe

the super waffle cafe

1620 shattuck avenue. between cedar and virginia
510.845.2233 www.guerillacafe.com
tue - fri 7a - 3p sat - sun 8a - 5p

opened in 2006. owners: andrea ali, keba konte and rachel konte
$: mc. visa
breakfast. lunch. brunch. first come, first served

east bay : berkeley : gourmet ghetto > **e22**

when my siblings and i were really good kids growing up, we would sometimes get a special treat: my father would make waffles for dinner. maybe it was a reward, or maybe he just had a craving. whichever, it gave me an unconditional love of butter and syrup on top of a golden brown confection. at *guerilla cafe* they make daily special waffles that hold up to my childhood memories. they even surpass them. these are the belgian variety, the type with the really deep pockets which hold even more of the good stuff. having one made me feel like a good kid again.

imbibe / devour:
guerrilla hot chocolate
red gold & green spritzers
waffle of the day
organic polenta porridge
grapefruit halves with honey
panini of the day
poached eggs with polenta
prosciutto sides

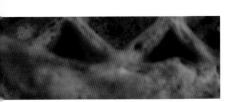

ici

ice cream and treat shop

2948 college avenue. corner of ashby
510.665.6054 www.ici-icecream.com
mon 2 - 9:30p tue - thu noon - 9:30p fri - sun noon - 10p

opened in 2006. owners / chefs: mary canales and mattea soreng
$: mc. visa
treats. coffee/tea. first come, first served

east bay : berkeley : elmwood >

when you see a cop car outside a donut place, it usually means the donuts are great. the same theory holds true when you see a line of people queued up outside an ice cream shop. *ici* means 'here' in french, and here is where you must be for ice cream. the accomplished kitchen at this white candybox festooned with signature curlicues creates frozen magic, with an assortment of delish flavors made daily. personally, i'm besotted with the housemade ice cream sandwiches. if you're not the waiting type, just look at the devour list below and you'll know *ici* is worth it.

imbibe / devour:
blue bottle coffee
hot chocolate
affogato
honey lavender ice cream
pink peppercorn ice cream
mango lime ice cream
lemon gingersnap ice cream sandwich
delicious shortbread

la taqueria

classic taco and burritos
2889 mission street. corner of 25th
415.285.7117
mon - sat 11a - 9p sun 11a - 8p

opened in 1973. owner: miquel jara
$ - $$: cash
lunch. dinner. first come, first served

sf : the mission > e24

here's a free tip. when a restaurant advertises in neon that they have the best of something in the world, don't believe them. unless, it's *la taqueria*. they proudly claim to have the best tacos and burritos in the world. and, they might just be right. for years, this mission street staple has been making, what many consider, sustenance they can't live without. everything here is made fresh and right before your eyes. the carnitas are just as i like, crispy and juicy. and the burritos, made without beans or rice, are pure meaty goodness wrapped in a carbolicious wrapper. yum.

imbibe / devour:
aquas frescas
horchata
chips with fresh-made salsa
tacos:
  al pastor
  carnitas
  chorizo
  carne asada

liguria bakery

legendary focaccia bakery
1700 stockton street. corner of filbert
415.421.3786
mon - fri 8a - 2p sat 7a - 2p sun 7a - noon

opened in 1911. owners: the soracco family
$: cash
bakery. first come, first served

sf : north beach > **e25**

FOCACCIA

PLAIN	$ 3.50
ONION	$ 3.50
PIZZA	$ 3.75
RAISIN	$ 3.75
GARLIC	$ 3.75
ROSEMARY	$ 4.00
MUSHROOM	$ 4.00
BLACK OLIVE	$ 4.00
ROSEMARY GARLIC	$ 4.00

CASH ONLY

wouldn't it be cool to throw a dinner party comprised of all the amazing foods you've discovered from your travels around the world? at my fantasy wing-dings, i would include the focaccia from *liguria bakery*. this family-run bakery has been making this savory bread here for almost one hundred years. you learn how to do it right in a century, and it shows. a hint about *liguria*: i suggest you visit early in the day because when they sell out, which they always do, they close their doors until the next morning. now on to my fantasy dessert course… mmm.

imbibe / devour:
focaccia:
  garlic
  plain
  raisin
  onion
  pizza
  olive
  mushroom

lovejoy's tea room

laid back high tea

1351 church street. corner of clipper
415.648.5895 www.lovejoystearoom.com
wed - sun 11a - 6p

opened in 2000. owners: muna nash and gillian briley
$ - $$: mc. visa
tea. lunch. treats. reservations recommended

lovejoy's tea room takes a californian, free-thinking approach and applies it to the staid tradition of high english tea. many of the traditions are still adhered to here: cheddar and chutney finger sandwiches, petits fours, and a perfectly brewed pot of tea. the place even looks like your eccentric british aunt's living room. but when you are served a pot of tea in a tea service with a peace sign on it, you realize this aunt has spent some time in the golden state. i love that they are a bit laid-back here, so much so that if you love your tea service… you can buy it and take it home.

imbibe / devour:
lemon barley water
taylor's tea room blend
scones with double devon cream
queen's tea
cucumber & cream cheese finger sandwiches
chicken apple-walnut salad sandwiches
ploughman's lunch
petits fours

RESERVED for Royalty

lucca delicatessen

classic italian deli and food store

2120 chestnut street. corner of steiner
415.921.7873 www.luccadeli.com
mon - fri 10a - 3p

opened in 1929. owners: paul bosco and linda bosco fioretti
$: mc. visa
lunch. grocery. first come, first served

sf : the marina > **e27**

in my past life, i was an art dealer. each spring the gallery would pack up the latest and greatest and bring it to the s.f. art expo. peddling spendy art to well-heeled clients may sound glam, but it had its downside—it was grueling. my pacifier was to go to *lucca* and pick up my antidote for feelings of self pity: the most delicious sandwich in the bay area, the italian combo on super sour. antidepressant hoagie in hand, i would sit and look at the golden gate bridge. i was soon transported out of my funk by the perfect concoction of meat, bread, mayo and the amazing scenery.

imbibe / *devour:*
san benedetto red orange soda
illy caffe
italian combo on extra sour bread
shrimp salad
the world's best fritatta
handmade ravioli
italian meatballs
cannoli

miette confiserie

dream candy store

449 octavia boulevard. between hayes and linden
415.626.6221 www.miette.com
mon - sat 11a - 7p sun 11a- 5p

opened in 2007. owners: meg ray and caitlin williams
$ - $$: all major credit cards accepted
treats. first come, first served

sf : hayes valley >

"who can take a rainbow, wrap it in a sigh? soak it in the sun and make a str'bry lemon pie?" sammy davis, jr. can't, but caitlin and meg can. they opened *miette confiserie* to satisfy all of our candy store fantasies. there are treats from around the world here and a load of great locally made sweets, too. all are displayed in giant jars and pretty stands which fortify the fantasy. the *confiserie* also has a sibling, *miette pâtisserie* which is located in the ferry building. their baked goods are a dream and are thankfully available here also... satisfying and delicious.

imbibe / devour:
rose geranium cotton candy
gimme sugar nougats
dream of caramels handmade caramels
charles chocolates
poco dolce
imported dutch licorice
miette french macarons & cupcakes
cloetta swedish candy bar

65

mission pie

delicious pie that rebuilds communities

2901 mission street. corner of 25th

415.282.4PIE / 415.282.1500 www.missionpie.com

mon - thu 7a - 9p fri 7a - 10p sat 8a - 10p sun 8a - 9p

opened in 2007. owner: karen heisler and joseph schuver

$: cash

lunch. coffee / tea. treats. first come, first served

sf : the mission > **e29**

Sweet Potato Pie
Slice – 3.50
Whole – 18.00

DESSERT PIE
organic fruit, nuts, b
SLICE OF PIE
MINI PIE
ITTY BITTY PIE
GALETTE
WHOLE PIE
PASTRIES
SCONES -SWEET &
MUFFINS
ISSION PIE Com

a guilty pleasure is something decadent that makes you feel just a wee bit sinful. to some, eating pie requires a few hail marys. but there's no need for penance at *mission pie*, whose vision is to inform and inspire people to know and take part in the food they eat. proceeds from pie sales here go to the non-profit organization, *the pie ranch*. so you get to eat delicious pie and help the community at the same time—it's a win-win! i suggest you show your philanthropy with a slice of the standout pecan pie.

imbibe / devour:
organic taylor maid farms coffee
organic columbia gorge fruit juices
pies:
  garlic & rosemary beef
  vegetable coconut curry
  walnut
  banana cream
  sweet potato

Banana Cream Pie
Slice – 3.50
Whole

nopa

a north of the pan handle hot spot

560 divisadero. corner of hayes
415.864.8643 www.nopasf.com
mon - sun 6p - 1a bar 5p - 1a

opened in 2006. owners: jeff hanak, allyson woodman and laurence jossel
$$: all major credit cards accepted
dinner. full bar. reservations recommended

sf : nopa > **e30**

whenever a new restuarant opens in my neighborhood, i become as jumpy as a flea and i feel as though i have to try to keep my grandiose expectations under wraps. the people who live near *nopa* must have felt like ticks at westminster dog show when a former bank and laundromat turned into this sexy and satisfying neighborhood hot spot. the food is super comfort-y, like the nine-hour bolognese with creamy polenta which i could easily eat most nights of the week, but the sexy atmosphere makes you feel all grown up like a prize-winning whippet.

imbibe / devour:
the old cuban cocktail
the ideal cocktail
lamb shank, dixie butter beans & crispy shallots
hamburger, pickled onions & fries
grilled asparagus with egg, capers & tarragon
nine-hour bolognese, creamy polenta & parmesan
flatbread with lamb sausage & mustard greens
almond cake, strawberries & whipped cream

nua

wine bar with exceptional mediterranean food
550 green street. between columbus and grant
415.433.4000 www.nuasf.com
sun - wed 6 - 10p thu - sat 6 - 11p

opened in 2007. owner: david white chef: anna bautista
$$ - $$$: all major credit cards accepted
dinner.   reservations recommended

sf : north beach >

eating and shopping is the career i have been training for my entire life. as a result, i have developed strong opinions about how things should be done. for example, i find it disappointing when wine bars have killer wine lists and try to pass off a hummus platter as an appropriate wine pairing. at *nua*, chef anna has written an inspired mediterranean menu to accompany an exceptional wine list. the peppers stuffed with brandade are sublime, the gambas al ajillo a triumph. but for dessert, the churros with spanish style hot chocolate are already legendary.

imbibe / devour:
01 castello della paneretta
domaine sigalas
piquillo peppers stuffed with brandade
gambas al ajillo
grilled chicken spiedini
housemade spicy italian sausage
rack of lamb with green garlic potato gratin
spiced churros with hot chocolate

on the bridge

yoshoku franco-japonaise cuisine
1581 webster street. 205 japan center. corner of post
415.922.7765 www.sfonthebridge.com
mon - sun 11:30a - 10p

opened in 1992. owner / chef: mitsuhiro nakamura
$ - $$: visa. mc
lunch. dinner. wine / beer. first come, first served

sf : japantown > **e32**

many countries adapt other countries' foods. take for example the chalupa extreme. nowhere will you find this in mexico, but here in the states we still refer to it as mexican food. another example is yoshoku style in japan. this is a food craze where western and european cuisines are japan-ified. most notable is the spaghetti where the sauce is replaced with such things as fish roe and nori. at *on the bridge*, which is literally located in the walkway over post street inside the japan center, they serve many delicious examples of yoshoku. go with an open mind and don't expect mexi-nuggets.

imbibe / *devour:*
calpico-hi cocktail
ume "plum": hi chu-hi cocktail
mentaiko spaghetti with cod roe
sansai spaghetti with vegetables
chicken lime
scallop curry
hamburger-steak japonaise
calamari & kimchi spaghetti

73

piccino

cute neighborhood pizza cafe

801 22nd street. corner of tennessee
415.824.4224 www.piccinocafe.com
mon - tue 7a - 3p wed - fri 7a - 9:30p sat 8a - 9:30p sun 8a - 3p

opened in 2006. owner / chefs: sheryl rogat and margherita stewart-sagan
\$ - \$\$: mc. visa
breakfast. lunch. dinner. coffee / tea. treats. wine / beer
first come, first served

sf : dogpatch >

piccino is a family restaurant. i don't mean salisbury steak and waitresses who call you "sugar." rather, dining here feels like having dinner with your family— if you like your relatives, that is. as i was taking these pictures at *piccino,* my neighboring table offered me friendly shooting tips and restaurant suggestions to check out in the city. the owners frequently stopped at all the tables and hugged entering customers. it's warm and embracing to feel so at home in a place that makes such wonderful food. sheryl and margherita, will you adopt me?

imbibe / devour:
bear republic brewery co. racer 5 ipa
domaine les pallieres rosé
asparagus, cracked egg & chili oil pizza
star route arugula & speck pizza
potato, garlic & parsley frittata
pasticcio (pancetta & green garlic bread pudding)
almond orange-blossom cake
cappuccino brûlée served with cookies

pizzaiolo

italian cuisine done right

5008 telegraph avenue. between 51st and 49th
510.652.4888 www.pizzaiolo.us
coffee and toast 7a - 11a dinner mon - sat 5:30p - 10p

opened in 2005. owner / chef: charlie hallowell
$$: all major credit cards accepted
dinner. full bar. coffee / tea. first come, first served

east bay : oakland : temescal >

i think that san franciscans don't like to cross the bay bridge for dinner. i understand it's a big, scary bridge that seems at odds with nature and filled with sleep-deprived truck drivers. but dear sf'ers, *pizzaiolo* is not only worth the drive, it's worth swimming across the bay. the meatball pizza is perfect in every way with a crust that is indefectible—it stands up to its toppings without getting soggy. and speaking of, the toppings are fab-u-awesome. mix this with the char from the wood-burning oven and you get pies that are worth a drive, swim. or maybe even a flight.

imbibe / devour:
the pizzaiolo cocktail
grapefruit daiquiri
rosemary pappardelle with pork ragu & peas
farro with georgia white shrimp & spinach
meatballs & red onion wood fire pizza
wild nettles & ricotta salata wood fire pizza
walnut, frangipane & rhubarb crostata

77

pizzeria delfina

pizza!!!

3611 18th street. between guerrero and dolores
415.437.6800 www.pizzeriadelfina.com
mon 5:30p - 10p tue - thu 11:30a - 10p fri 11:30 - 11p
sat noon - 11p sun noon - 10p

opened in 2005. owners: craig and anne stoll
$ - $$: all major credit cards accepted
lunch. dinner. wine / beer. first come, first served

sf : the mission > **e35**

everywhere you turn in san francisco these days, there seems to be a new pizza place. this is a city of lucky people: you have great wine, access to amazing produce, and now loads of amazing pizza places. the only difficult thing left to figure out is which one to frequent. as an offshoot of the unanimously loved *delfina*, *pizzeria delfina* almost seems like it's been around forever, though it only opened two years ago. if you haven't been yet, try the broccoli di ciccio to start and follow up with a pizza. but don't forget the bellwether ricotta cannoli—they are supremo.

imbibe / devour:
boylan rootbeer
lambrusco reggiano
asparagus with sieved egg & lemon vinaigrette
grilled fennel with bottarga
broccoli raab, ricotta & oven dried tomato pizza
cherrystone clams, tomato & pecorino pizza
tomato sauce, cream, basil & parmigiano pizza
bellwether ricotta cannoli

range

neighborhood bistro with excellent cocktails

842 valencia street. between 19th and 20th
415.282.8283 www.rangesf.com
sun - thu 5:30 - 10p fri - sat 5:30p - 11p

opened in 2005. owners: cameron and phil west chef: phil west
$$: visa. mc
dinner. full bar. reservations recommended

sf : the mission > **e36**

the name of the signature on my royalty checks is ms. kaie wellman. she is the tastemaker and all-around big cheese of the *eat.shop* enterprise. when i get instructions from her, i follow. fortunately, she never steers me wrong. she instructed me to go to *range* and said that i would love it. right and right. *range* is exactly what i love in a restaurant: a helpful, confident staff, a magician behind the bar and food that is flawlessly prepared with loads of interesting flavors, but with none of those extra bells and whistles that make my eyes begin to roll. thanks, kaie and *range*.

imbibe / devour:
the long goodbye cocktail
asparagus with poached egg comte
 & breadcrumbs
whiskey & brown sugar glazed spare ribs
canadian cod with spring vegetables
fromage blanc stuffed artichokes with beluga lentils
mint chocolate ice cream puffs with
 bourbon chocolate sauce

ritual coffee

artisanal roaster
tm: 1026 valencia street. between 21st and 22nd. 415.641.1024
tb: 1634 jerrold avenue. in flora grubb gardens. 415.694.6448
www.ritualroasters.com
(see website for hours)

opened in 2005. owners: eileen hassi
$: mc. visa
coffee / tea. treats. online shopping. first come, first served

i went to *ritual coffee* probably four times before i talked to someone about taking pictures for this book. this place is hopping: whether it was eight in the morning or five in the evening, it didn't matter—there was always a line of people waiting for a steaming hot cappuccino or a circus-colored cupcake. don't be timid; the reason it's crowded is because it's fantastic. just dive in, snag a table and enjoy your delicious coffee while you listen to the sound of the coffee roasters whirling away and you watch the world come and go.

imbibe | devour:
clover made drip coffee
macchiato
mocha
cream soda
peanut butter cookies
sugar sprinkle cookies
tiny carrot cake cupcakes
caramel-nut bar cookies

ESPRESSO 1.50 2
MACCHIATO 1.75 2.25
CAPPUCCINO 2.25 2.75
LATTE 2.25 2.75

roadside bbq

3751 geary boulevard. corner of 2nd
415.221.7427 www.roadside-bbq.com
sun - thu 11:30a - 10p fri - sun 11:30a - 11p

opened in 2006. owner: randy kaplan
$ - $$: mc. visa
lunch. dinner. first come, first served

sf : inner richmond >

the day i visited *roadside bbq*, i was there for an early lunch and there were only a couple of other tables of diners. i sat by one filled with four friends, all engineers, who had met to have a weekly food critique. i sat back, enjoying my pulled-pork sandwich, so i could eavesdrop better. they evaluated the smoke vs. the sweet and debated the bbq's attributes. something struck me as wonderful that these guys were discussing their food with such considered eloquence. and then i remembered this was s.f. after all, where good food is as much a sport as a sunday football game.

imbibe / devour:
sweet tea
memphis pulled-pork sandwich
mr. brisket
the iceberg wedge
texas brisket
mac 'n' cheese
garlic fries with happy mouth spice
coconut banana cream pie

saigon sandwiches

vietnamese sandwiches
560 larkin. corner of eddy
415.474.5698
mon - sat 6a - 6p sun 7a - 5p

opened in 1980
$: cash
lunch. grocery. treats. first come, first served

sf : the tenderloin >

i've never been to asia, except for the brief moment that i closed my eyes at *saigon sandwich* in the tenderloin. with eyes closed, all the elements were there. the sounds, the disorientation, the borderline chaos, the super-affordability and the smells of exotic spices and citrus. this could either scare you away or send you sprinting for larkin street. i suggest the sprint as the bahn mi here are great. crusty, warm bread accented with the bright flavors of cilantro, lime and jalapeño and the meat of your choice. add a squirt of asian mayo and, whoosh, you're in hanoi.

imbibe / devour:
yeo's sodas
sandwiches:
  roast chicken
  roast pork
  meatball pork
  fanci pork
  pate
mung bean cakes

sam's grill and seafood restaurant

a historical classic

374 bush street. corner of belden
415.421.0594 www.belden-place.com/samsgrill
mon - fri 11a - 9p

opened in 1867. owners: the seput family
$$-$$$: all major credit cards accepted
lunch. dinner. reservations recommended

sf : financial district > **e40**

i like to keep a toe, eye, or whatever on the past to remember how we have gotten to where we are today. *sam's grill* is a reminder of what restaurants used to be. there may be new things here like electricity, but since opening in this space, *sam's* appears to have not changed much. small booths, like train dining compartments, are booked for private lunches. dishes like mock turtle soup and fresh abalone meuniere are served alongside classics like filet of sole. in this trend-obsessed culture, *sam's* reminds us that new is not the only answer.

imbibe / devour:
ferrari-carano fume blanc
freeman pinot noir
clam cocktail
pacific yearling oyster cocktail
hearts of romaine with red beans
mock turtle soup
deviled crab á la sam
pecan pie

sea salt

sustainable seafood

2512 san pablo avenue. between dwight and parker
510.883.1720 www.seasaltrestaurant.com
mon - fri 11:30a - 10p sat - sun 10:30a - 10p

opened in 2005. owners: haig and cindy krikorian chef: anthony paone
$$ - $$$: all major credit cards accepted
lunch. dinner. weekend brunch. reservations recommended

east bay : west berkeley > e41

people are slowly coming around to being more environmentally conscious. whether we should thank al gore or the new beach-front resort property in the arctic is beside the point—this movement is gaining strength. it only makes sense that this newfound awareness carries over to the restaurant industry. at *sea salt* they are committed to sustainability as well as innovation and healthy eating—this is doing that right thing, done incredibly well. the 'bahn mi' sandwich made with bbq eel is a fusion of cuisines that is perfection. i think a new term is in order: eco-licious.

imbibe / devour:
falernum martini
eye of the hawk draft beer
daily oysters
bbq eel 'banh mi' sandwich
steamed lobster on a torpedo roll
cornmeal & spice-crusted halibut
pan-seared loch duart salmon
peanut butter brownie sundae

shanghai dumpling king

soup dumplings!
3319 balboa street. between 34th and 35th
415.387.2088
sun - thu 10:30a - 9:15p fri - sat 10a - 9:30p

opened in 2005. owners: kuang lu and bing huang
$: mc. visa
lunch. dinner. first come, first served

sf : outer richmond > **e42**

i could solely eat dumplings for the rest of my life. *shanghai dumpling king* serves many varieties including the rarely found soup type. as soft and delicate as an egg without its shell, the precious packge is picked up in a spoon. pricking the wrapper releases a few teaspoons of hot nourishing soup from its dough wrapper. quickly, either sip or eat the dumpling in one big gulp. mmmm, i am ready to commit to my new dumpling lifestyle, especially if i can define donuts as dumplings.

imbibe / devour:
hot tea
hung zhou crab & pork steamed dumplings
beijing-style boiled chive dumplings
shanghai-style vermicelli soup
rice dumplings with wine filling
tread bread
salt duck
long life peach dumpling

sketch

ice cream and treat shop
1809a 4th street. between hearst and virginia
510.665.5650 www.sketchicecream.com
sun - thu noon - 6p fri - sat noon - 8p

opened in 2004. owners: eric shelton and ruthie planas-shelton
$: cash only
treats. first come, first served

east bay : berkeley : 4th street > **e43**

eric and ruthie feel that all great things start with a sketch, hence the name of their popular ice cream shop. i completely agree, but also feel that a lot of great things begin with sugar. for example, the burnt caramel ice cream starts with sugar. it's then cooked until it reaches the color of a model in a bain du soleil ad. when cream is added and the whole thing is frozen, it turns from a sketch to a masterpiece. other master works available at *sketch* are the earl 'great' tea ice cream and the incredible cookies.

imbibe / devour:
flavors:
  earl grey tea
  strauss yogurt
  lychee
  burnt caramel
  dark chocolate
  jasmine tea granita
housemade cookies & cakes

sKetCh
ice cream

sophia cafe

middle eastern cafe

1247 solano avenue. corner of masonic
510.526.8663 www.sophia-cafe.com
sun - fri 11a - 9p

opened in 2003. owner: moti dagan
$: all major credit cards accepted
lunch. dinner. treats. first come, first served

east bay : albany > **e44**

i have no idea how to make baklava, but i know what i like it to taste like. it should be light, yet substantial. rose-scented layers should retain their fragile crispness despite being imbued with light honey syrup. and of course, pistachios and walnuts must play an important role keeping the sweet notes in check as to not overwhelm the pastry's delicate balance. at *sophia cafe* they make baklava just the way i like it. and after i'm done with my treat, i'm sure i'll have room for the fantastic falafel and eggplant salad.

imbibe / devour:
limonata
potato & onion bourekas
grilled eggplant salad
moroccan cigars
mediterranean meatballs
falafel sandwich
poppy hamantashan
baklava

spork

modern american comfort foods
1058 valencia. between 21st and 22nd
415.643.5000 www.sporksf.com
tue - thu 6 - 10p fri - sat 6 - 11p

opened in 2007. owners: neil jorgensen and bruce binn chef: bruce binn
$$: mc. visa
dinner. wine / beer. first come, first served

sf : the mission > e45

a spork is a spoon/fork combo if you didn't know already. this funky, utilitarian tool of questionable origin is the namesake of this brand-new mission hot spot. chef bruce certainly has a sense of humor with his takes on classic american comfort foods. from the housemade chips and caviar which is super clever and delicious, to the in-side-out burger with just the right amount of goodies piled high on top of its cattywampus meat-and-bread foundation. this is not quite finger food, and not quite silverplate fare either—it's all perfect for using a spork!

imbibe / devour:
domaine des baumard chenin blanc
witness tree vineyard pinot noir
cream of champignon soup with housemade rolls
housemade chips & caviar
in-side-out burger with smashed fries
lazy ravioli
martha's chopped vineyard
pot brownie

swan oyster depot

classic oyster and seafood lunchbar
1517 polk street. between sacramento and california
415.673.1101
mon - sat 8a - 5:30p

opened in 1912. owners: jim, steve and tom sancimino
$$: cash
breakfast. lunch. dinner. first come, first served

sf : russian hill > **e46**

i naturally gravitate toward certain places when i do these guides. for example, i have to sample almost every donut shop i pass. also, i have come to realize i love places with a long history, places that readily show their years of longevity. *swan oyster bar* pulled me in like a boat to the point bonita lighthouse. with its selection of fresh seafood on display in the window, i hardly needed to look further. then i saw the fresh oysters being shucked and bowls of steaming clam chowder being enjoyed by both grandmothers and hipsters at a long counter. i was hooked, line and sinker.

imbibe / devour:
stella artois
sineann pinot gris
boston clam chowder
blue point, miyagi & kumamoto oysters
smoked salmon
cracked crab
lobster salad
shrimp cocktail

tamarindo

antojeria mexicana

468 8th street. between washington and broadway
510.444.1944 www.tamarindoantojeria.com
lunch mon - fri 11a - 3p sat 10a - 3p
dinner mon 5 - 9p tue - thu 5 - 9:30p fri - sat 5 - 10p

opened in 2005. owner / chef: gloria dominguez owner: alfonso dominguez
$$: all major credit cards accepted
lunch. dinner. brunch. wine / beer. first come, first served

east bay : old oakland > e47

something is brewing in downtown oakland. ten years ago, when I first visited, there wasn't much in the way of incredible food. this was still a place a bit down on its luck, and foodies stayed north. much can change in a decade. take for example, *tamarindo*, a spectacular new mexican restaurant. either the city just needed an extraordinary tamal oaxaqueño, or sopecitos surtidos, or it was just oakland's time to shine in the foodie spotlight. i think it has a lot to do with the dominguez family. with vision, devotion, and an extraordinary flan they are turning old oakland into a food destination.

imbibe / devour:
housemade sangria
aquas frescas
sopecitos surtidos
tres ceviche
tamal oaxaqueño tostaditas de tinga poblana
cochinita pibil
flan de coco
crepas con cajeta

tartine bakery

famous bakery for good reason

600 guerrero street. corner of 18th
415.487.2600 www.tartinebakery.com
mon 8a - 7p tue - wed 7:30a - 7p
thu - fri 7:30a - 8p sat 8am - 8p sun 9a - 8p

opened in 2002. owners / chefs: chad robertson and elisabeth prueitt
$ - $$: all major credit cards accepted
breakfast. lunch. coffee. treats. first come, first served

sf : the mission > **e48**

it seems that everyone from coast to coast knows of the formidable *tartine bakery*. so on my first visit here, i half expected baked items so unique that they would change my world.   but all i saw were the classics: croissants, tarts, breads, scones and sandwiches. jaded author that i am, i thought big deal. then i tasted the coconut cream tart. once i picked my jaw off the ground, i quickly ordered a fragipane croissant. it was truly spectacular. but how is it that this genius pastry was made with the same flour, sugar and butter that everyone else uses? only chad and elisabeth know.

imbibe / devour:
organic coffee
fresh-squeezed juice
morning buns with cinnamon & orange
humboldt fog goat cheese on walnut bread
croque monsieur
lemon meringue cake
devils food cake
lemon almond poundcake

the alembic

bar with excellent whiskey selection and eats

1725 haight street. corner of cole
415.666.0822 www.alembicbar.com
mon - thu 5p - midnight fri - sun noon - midnight bar until 2a

opened in 2006. owner: david mclean chef: eddie blyden
$ - $$: all major credit cards accepted
lunch. dinner. full bar. first come, first served

sf : the haight > e49

if your color of preference is brown when it comes to liquor and your evening calls for quality over quantity, then *the alembic* is just your ticket. they feature an impressive selection of scotches, bourbons, and also old-school cocktails like the sazerac and pisco sour. and make sure to get some devour to go with your imbibe. the lamb sliders are perfect little nuggets of delectable-ness in between sips of an icy pimms cup. a meal like this can only be finished with, you guessed it, a manhattan float. mmmm, yummy and just a bit drunky.

imbibe / devour:
drinks:
  the 'mary poppins'
  sazerac
  pimms cup
lamb sliders
tempura of okra and local fish
buttermilk fried chicken quesadilla
herb spice-dusted frites

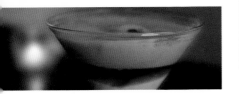

the blue plate

new american

3218 mission street. corner of valencia
415.282.6777 www.blueplatesf.com
mon - thu 6 - 10p fri - sat 6 - 10:30p

opened in 1999. chef and owner: cory obenour
$$: all major credit cards accepted
dinner. wine / beer. reservations recommended

sf : outer mission > **e50**

when a friend told me about the legendary meatloaf at *the blue plate*, i remained skeptical. i had developed formidable ideas about loaves of meat since my childhood love affair began with the stuff. sitting at the bar, i watched this mythological meatloaf being served to table after table. after a splendid primer of seared scallops, my loaf arrived. i took a bite. damn, this was otherworldly—tender and hearty, zesty and comforting. i hadn't known i was feeling so fragile until a wave of consoling bliss blanketed me with happiness and peace. happy sigh.

imbibe / devour:
domaine serene yamhill cuvée
hearts of romaine, bacon, avocado & tomatoes
pan-seared scallops parsnip puree & crispy leeks
house-cured sardines, hearts of palm & oranges
cornflake-crusted duck liver schnitzel
blue plate meatloaf & mashed potatoes
painted hills ribeye, herb fries & aioli
strawberry rhubarb pie with mascarpone ice cream

the candy store

like your favorite candy store from childhood

1507 vallejo street. corner of polk
415.921.8000 www.thecandystoresf.com
tue - sun 10a - 7p

opened in 2007. owners: diane and brian campbell
$: all major credit cards accepted
treats. first come, first served

sf : russian hill >

as a poor, young farm child, i would scrape together my pennies, jump on my schwinn one-speed and ride five miles to the small town of malta, illinois. i would head to *spot-lite*, the local general store, and buy fun dip and zotz. these trips made me feel adult and independent, and p.s., i loved artificial grape flavoring. diane had a similar experience from her childhood, so she dreamed of recreating that store. voila! *the candy store* was born. with an unsurpassed selection of old-school candies along with more modern day types, i left the shop looking for my schwinn.

imbibe / devour:
zotter chocolates
fun dip
l. c. good handmade lollipops
james salt-water taffy
marzipan fruit
malo cups
zotz
chocolate olives

the front porch

southern comfort food

65a 29th street. between san jose and mission
415.695.7800 www.thefrontporchsf.com
mon - sun 5p - midnight food 5:30 - 10:30p

opened in 2006. owners: josey white and kevin cline chef: sarah kirnon
$$: all major credit cards accepted
dinner. wine / beer. reservations recommended

sf : outer mission > e52

there is a rock 'n' roll vibe at *the front porch*. well, maybe it's more rockabilly with some reggae beats. furnished in vintage-chic, the comfortable atmosphere makes me want to drink. hmm, that doesn't sound right—the point is, you know you'll have a good time here eating southern comfort food. miss ollie's fried chicken is rib-sticking good and is accompanied by grits and black-eyed peas. if that doesn't sound fun enough for you, on first sundays during the summer they do caribbean bbq: steak, chicken and fish with west indian sides. partay!

imbibe / devour:
el toro brewing poppy jasper amber ale
santenay gravieres
west indian chips
plantain cakes with house-cured wild salmon
miss ollie's fried chicken
escoveitch fish with coconut red beans & rice
caribbean bbq
fresh beignets

tokyo fish

awesome fresh fish and asian food market
1220 san pablo avenue. corner of harrison
510.524.7243
mon - sat 9a - 6p

opened in 1963. owners: larry fujita and lee nakamura
$ - $$: mc. visa
groceries. treats. first come, first served

east bay : albany > **e53**

tokyo fish is really a grocery store, though it has no resemblance to your local safeway. with nary a can of starkist in sight, this is one of the best selections of fresh fish available anywhere in the bay area. many s.f. citizens make a regular saturday daytrip here in search of the freshest of the fresh fish. if the saba, maguro and hamachi aren't alluring enough, try the wall of sake. this is an asian-food fantasyland, complete with packets of things with flavors i don't understand but always love. i suggest you come to explore.

imbibe / devour:
the freshest of fresh fish
fresh sardines
crab croquettes
cans of sapporo
huge sake collection
fresh wasabi root
zippy's chili
pocky

true sake

premier sake shop

560 hayes street. between octavia and laguna
415.355.9555 www.truesake.com
mon - sat noon - 7p sun 11a - 6p

opened in 2003. owner: beau timken
$$: all major credit cards accepted
sake. online shopping. first come, first served

sf : hayes valley >

like many great ideas, *true sake* started with a flash of inspiration. beau was drinking inferior hot sake in a restaurant one day when a group of japanese fishermen pointed out to him the charms and subtleties that could exist in sake, though not in the one he was drinking. sake soon became his passion and he began to learn all that he could. four years ago he opened the first u.s. store devoted entirely to sake. he is committed to spreading the word about the diversity and range of sakes and having people truly experience this ancient and refined libation. *kampai*!

imbibe / devour:
sakes:
  wakatake onikoroshi
  kaika nama
  gokyo nama
  harushika tokimeki sparkling
  hou hou shu
  ken "sword" limited-edition release
  sawanoi "fountain of tokyo"

underdog

organic hot dog stand
1634 irving street. between 17th and 18th
415.665.8881
mon - sun 11:30a - 9:30p

opened in 2007. owners: rizza punzalan and max leung
$ - $$: cash
lunch. dinner. first come, first served

sf : outer sunset > **e55**

the availability of organic ingredients and the focus on sustainability on the left coast is unsurpassed. in just a few short years, organic food, once rare, is readily available. but there are still a few food items from back in the days when eating chemicals was de rigeur that haven't successfully made the leap to organic. hello *underdog*, where tater tots and hot dogs are all made of organic ingredients, as are the ketchup, bun, relish... everything. goodbye unhealthy junk food, *underdog* is here to save the day.

imbibe / devour:
honest tea
purity organic juices
dogs:
  the underdog
  the fire-roasted red pepper
  the veggie kielbasa
organic tater-tots
mission pies

vik's chaat shop

south indian chaat restaurant
726 allston way. corner of 4th
510.644.4432 www.vikschaatcorner.com
tue - sun 11a - 6p

opened in 1989. owners: vinod and indira chopra
$: all major credit cards accepted
lunch. dinner. treats. first come, first served

east bay : berkeley : 4th street >

DESSERTS
RASMALAI . . .
GULAB JAMUN .
ROLLS 1LB . . .
MIXED MITHAI 1LB . .
MIXED MITHAI BOX . . .
CASHEW BOX BIG . .

vik's is as much a vacation as a restaurant. it's a sensory exploration of southern india where the smells, sounds and experiences are vastly different that what we are used to here in the states. the large, dimly lit room is accompanied by a loud-speaker announcing the names of the recipients of freshly made masala dosas, the size of golden rolls of christmas wrapping paper. then someone walks by with a steaming bhatura cholle that looks like an oversized whoopee cushion. whoa. aren't you happy that you took this trip?

imbibe / devour:
thumbs up soda
chai
masala dosa
lamb baida roti
samosa cholle
mixed vegetable pakoras
dhokla
vada sambar

walzwerk

east german bar and restaurant

381 south van ness avenue. between 14th and 15th
415.551.7181 www.walzwerk.com
mon - sun 5:30p - 10p

opened in 1999. owner: christiane schmidt
$$: all major credit cards accepted
dinner. wine / beer. reservations accepted for parties of four or more

sf : the mission > **e57**

it is interesting to check out the people that different restaurants attract. congregated at walzwerk was a beer lovin', bed-headed bohemian crowd. as this is an east german restaurant, this "for the people" vibe made sense to me. here you'll find no pretense, great beer served in signature glassware, and tasty food. there seemed to be ample amounts of gregariousness at the simple wooden tables, and i half expected a rousing verse of "auferstanden aus ruinen" to begin any minute. so what did i do? i quoted "cabaret," and was immediately welcomed into the fun.

imbibe / devour:
kostritzer schwarzbier
weltenburg amber
potato pancake with chive sour cream
jager schnitzel with spaetzle
saurbraten with potato dumpling & cabbage
baked cod with chard & leeks
"cold dog"
homemade chocolate pudding

weird fish

fish-fry joint

2193 mission street. corner of 18th
415.863.4744 www.weirdfishsf.com
daily 9a - 10p fri and sat open late

opened in 2006. owner: timothy holt
$ - $$: mc. visa
breakfast. lunch. dinner. first come, first served

sf : the mission > **e58**

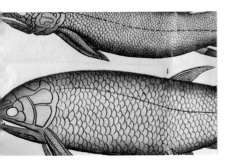

like an english pub mixed with a midwestern fish-fry joint run by a hipster, *weirdfish* is as much fun as it is satisfying. tucked away in a tiny spot in the mission, it literally has something for everyone: vegan fish and chips, fried green beans, crab louie! *weirdfish* is the kind of place you pray will open in your own neighborhood. it fills that bottomless niche of wanting a restaurant that's laid back, not too expensive, yet with great food. and just to note, *weirdfish* really isn't weird at all—just good ole' tasty fun.

imbibe / devour:
negra modelo
moinette brune unfiltered
jane's old-school crab louie salad
fried green beans with aioli
sautéed calamari
tilapia fish & chips
almond dijon-crusted trout with mashed yams
chocolate turtle cake

zuni cafe

the classic s.f. bistro
1658 market street. between gough and franklin
415.552.2522 www.zunicafe.com
tue - sat 11:30a - midnight sun 11a - 11p

opened in 1979. owners: judy rodgers and gilbert pilgram chef: judy rodgers
$$ - $$$: all major credit cards accepted
lunch. dinner. full bar. reservations recommended

sf : civic center > **e59**

in each city, i always have a favorite restaurant that i must visit to make my stay complete. in san francisco, my must-go-to restaurant is *zuni*. whether i stop in for the hamburger at lunch or their fabled roast chicken at dinner, or whether i just go to enjoy a drink in the afternoon at the stand-up copper bar—i always nothing but love feelings for *zuni*. whenever i've been there, it feels like i've spent quality time with family that i don't see very often. i leave the re-union feeling great but also already dreaming of the next time i'll get to visit.

imbibe / devour:
campari & soda
marinated leeks with hard-cooked egg
the famous zuni caesar
asparagus soup with mint & lemon oil
yellowfin tuna grilled rare with white beans
roasted chicken for two
espresso granita with whipped cream

notes

eat

shop

826 valencia

pirate supplies and more
826 valencia street. between 19th and 20th
415.642.5905 www.826valencia.org/store
mon - sun noon - 6p

opened in 2002. owners: the community
all major credit cards accepted
online shopping

sf : the mission > **s01**

did you know that the last pirate hanged in the united states was captain nathaniel gordon in 1862? since then, pirates have enjoyed relative peace and prosperity, so much so that they have their very own store right in the middle of the mission. if you're a pirate, *826 valencia* is where you can stock up on new spy glasses, flags, eye patches and of course lard. this flourishing community of pirates is philanthropic too. they donate all of their proceeds to the 826 writing project which is housed in the back of the shop. nice pirates.

covet:
eye patch
spy glass
message in a bottle
pirate flag
deck prism
karl is king t's
mcsweeny's t's
826 quarterly

addison endpapers

artifacts and artistry
886 colusa avenue. corner of solano
510.525.2904
11a - 6p mon - sat

opened in 1996. owners: julie, marina and geneva addison
all major credit cards accepted
custom orders

east bay : berkeley > **s02**

while i was eating and shopping my way around the east bay, a small shop, aglow like a field of spring tulips, lured me in. once i entered, i realized i was in *addison endpapers*, a place my friend had told me about but i could never locate. this place is captivating with its unusually elegant treasures and rareties. the shop is stocked with personally selected flea-market finds as well as handmade creations gorgeously produced by the addison family. i had to pinch myself to assure this magic spot was not a figment of my imagination.

covet:
hand-silkscreened ribbons
antique real silver embroidery thread
handmade silk flowers
handmade letterpress boxes
handmade lanterns
french flea-market rings
antique fabrics
old french tableware

al's attire

hand-tailored, custom clothes
1314 grant avenue. corner of vallejo
415.693.9900 www.alsattire.com
mon - sat 10a - 7p sun noon - 6p

opened in 1984. owner: al ribaya
all major credit cards accepted
custom designs

sf : north beach > **s03**

is your wardrobe the food equivalent of oatmeal? is your idea of spicy... mayonnaise? if so, read on because you need help. *al's attire* can make you the beau or belle of the ball—it's part bond street haberdashery, part hollywood stylist. with an impressive collection of vintage fabrics and buttons, everything in the shop is 100% al's vision; he makes clothing designed for your inner rock star. believe me, there's no other clothing like al's; it's truly bespoke and one of a kind. once you've had clothing made to fit, you'll never go back to off-the-rack.

covet:
custom navy blazer
circa #2 hat
the parkview coat
the linda dress
ms. bogart
newsboy hat
double-breasted mac pea coat
vintage fabric & buttons

135

alabaster

597 hayes street. corner of laguna
415.558.0482 www.alabastersf.com
tue - sat 11a - 6p sun noon - 5p or by appointment

opened in 1997. owner: nelson bloncourt
all major credit cards accepted
design services

sf : hayes valley > **s04**

alabaster, the stone, is an exquisite, soft and translucent marble-like substance. if you have ever seen a lamp made from this mineral, you can confirm that its glow is warm and seems to have mystical qualities. like its namesake, *alabaster*, the store, is exquiste and warm. a collection of hand-picked items from lighting to antiques is a treasure-trove for the home as nelson has an eye for items the graceful and exotic. there's a quietness here that i love—it seems to be an expression of nelson's artful restraint and it's a welcome calm in the big city.

covet:
vintage model sailboats
santa maria novella products
r & y augousti furniture
mercury glass antiques
andrew fisher coquillage spoons
alabaster lamps
fortuny purses
scrimshaw bone dragonfly & butterfly

alla prima

high-end lingerie store with expertise in fitting

1420 grant avenue. corner of green. 415.397.4077
539 hayes street. corner of octavia. 415.864.8180
www.allaprimalingerie.com
tue - sat 11a - 7p sun noon - 5p

opened in 1998. owners: maggie crystal and yolaida durán
all major credit cards accepted
custom orders

sf : north beach / hayes valley > s05

lingerie is an area for which i have no authority. for fried foods, i'm the expert, but for bras and panties, i must confer with my board of trusted experts. these connoisseurs of frilly foundations say *alla prima* is the best in the bay area because they not only have an incredible selection of high end dainties, but maggie and yolaida are fitting experts. not sure of your bra size? they'll take care of that and fit you in the perfect support. considering you have to wear those things around all day, i think this seems like helpful information.

covet:
andres sarda
eres
dolce & gabbana
mary jo bruno
hanky panky
gigi by underwriters
karen luu
jimmy jane

139

arch

amusing tools and serious toys for art and drafting

99 missouri street. corner of 17th
415.433.2724 www.archsupplies.com
mon - fri 9a - 6p sat noon - 5p

opened in 1978. owner: susie coliver
all major credit cards accepted

sf : potrero hill > **s06**

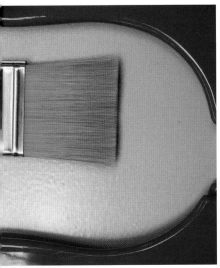

i have a few books up my sleeve. aside from the future *eat.shop guides* in the pipeline, i plan to write a self-help book titled, *make it yourself, laggard*. catchy, isn't it? i'm writng it because i feel like folks are too removed from the activity of making things. people, you need to get your scissors and gluesticks out and make a mess. don't have any? then march on over to *arch* where you will no doubt be inspired by the papers, brushes and everything else. not only will you feel rewarded by your burst of d.i.y., you might be surprised at what you create.

covet:
le corbu stencils
extensive rapidograph selection
da vinci brushes
pentagram calendars
koh-i-noor electric erasers
hishou japanese rubberband airplanes
radiometer
every color pen, pencil & marker imaginable

area

curated home and garden designs

540 jackson street. between columbus and montgomery
415.989.2732 www.areasanfrancisco.com
tue - fri 11a - 7p sat 10a - 6p

opened in 2005. owner: john giacomazzi
all major credit cards accepted
online shopping. design services

sf : jackson square > **s07**

what makes a home design and garden store stand out from the hordes of others is a strong point of view and personal attention. we can all go to design web-sites and order all kinds of stuff, but hey, why do it when there are stores like *area*? john takes his eagle eye for details, and nonstop passion for beauty, and scours the ends of the earth. i may seem zealous, but there are so many amazing items here, from marie christophe palerme lamps to rani arabella's cashmere throws. these are not ubiquitous design items but gorgeous works of art intended to refine your life.

covet:
casa de famillia water vessel
miller et bertaux fragrances
rani arabella cashmere throw
marie christophe palerme lamp
atlantico solid wood furniture
niche modern pendant lights
sakai toki trading ceramics
bunaco bamboo bowl

aria

furnishings and antiques

1522 grant avenue. between union and filbert
415.433.0219
mon - sun 11a - 6p

opened in 1995. owner: bill haskell
cash only
custom orders

sf : north beach > s08

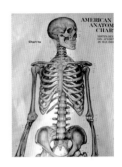

one of my favorite pastimes is to spend the day digging through treasures at a paris flea market. when you discover a really good market, you feel like you just threw snake eyes at the craps table. *aria* gives me that same 'hit the jackpot feeling.' here you'll find goods imported from european flea markets without having to sift through the undesirable items like dirty tupperware or stained blankets. everything has a bit of old european flair and a patina that only the old country can impart on its goods. visiting *aria* regularly is like having your own personal slot machine.

covet:
antique brass buttons
french school charts & maps
vintage botanical prints
french dice
antique lamps
leather club chair
antique lasts
old french calling cards

article pract

accoutrements for the stylish knitter

5010 telegraph avenue. between 49th and 51st
510.595.7875 www.articlepract.com
tue - thu 11a - 7p fri - sun 11a - 6p

opened in 2002. owner: christina stork
all major credit cards accepted

east bay : oakland : temescal > **s09**

the knitting revolution didn't pass me by. i jumped on the bandwagon quickly and became addicted to knitting's spellbinding qualities. but sometimes trying to find a knitting store aimed at my taste and not my grandmother's hasn't always been easy. *article pract* fits my niche just perfectly with its terrific selection of yarns and notions from hither and yon. it's much more japanese style than county fair here, where you could find materials for a stylish scarf rather than yarn for a crocheted budweiser hat. tell granny to drink her buds elsewhere. this store's for you.

covet:
yarns:
   debbie bliss silks
   regia sock yarn
   habu wool
   anny blatt
   burl spun
mother-of-pearl buttons
takumi bamboo needles

august

contemporary clothing and accessories

5410 college avenue. corner of manilla
510.652.2711 www.augustshop.com
mon - sun 11a - 6p

opened in 2005. owners: erin scott and louesa roebuck
all major credit cards accepted

east bay : oakland : rockridge > **s10**

the fact that august is the hottest month is a great clue to the quality of this smokin' oakland boutique. along one side of the beautiful gallery-like space, a shelf holds stacks of some of the most sought-after denim available. but *august* is no one trick-pony. sizzling designs from rogan, dagmar and kristensen du nord confirm that this is the best place for gorgeously fashion-forward clothing in the east bay. whether you want to dress-down with jeans or way, way up with a fabulous hache piece, *august* is somewhere to frequent all year long.

covet:
dagmar clothing
rogan clothing
gerard tully rings
jean shop wallets
gerard tully rings
maison martin margiela shoes
melanie dison shoes
hache

149

birch

gorgeous floral arrangements and objects for your home

3263a sacramento street. corner of presidio
415.922.4724 www.birchsf.com
tue - sat 10a - 6p

opened in 2007. owners: torryne choate and erin rosenow
all major credit cards accepted
custom orders

sf : presidio heights > s11

when i met caitlin from *miette* i knew she was a woman in the know, in other words a resource to pilfer. i quizzed her with a few style questions and she easily passed, so i decided that she could become a trusted source. she started with a few obvious places and then began to warm up. "you have to go to *birch* because the specimens of flowers are flawless," she noted and "they make these standing bouquets that are so sophisticated and elegant. the best in town." i thanked her and rushed to *birch* where i discovered caitlin was right on, *birch* is fantastic.

covet:
standing bouquets
perfect poppies
incredible parrot tulips
andrew de witt ceramics
cowshed vegetarian products
glassy baby votives
stop talking cards
bruno munari 'drawing a tree'

151

cactus jungle

cacti nursery and garden

1509 4th street. between cedar and jones
510.558.8650 www.cactusjungle.com
wed - mon 10a - 5p (closed in january)

opened in 2002. owners: peter lipson and hap hollibaugh
all major credit cards accepted
custom orders. design services

east bay : berkeley : 4th street > s12

let's face it, we are all busy. life sometimes takes so much time we forget to take care of the little details like changing the kitty litter, returning the borat dvd and watering the plants. i used to have these problems but then i had a eureka moment... buy cacti. these water-sipping succulents are not only exotic and intriguing to look at but also fit my absentminded tendencies. at *cactus jungle* you'll find a comprehensive selection of all things drought tolerant along with loads of helpful suggestions. now, i have time to watch that borat wrestling scene one more time.

covet:
aloe tenuior
raphionacme flanaganii
macodes petula
hoya compacta variegata
echinopsis tersheckii
echinopsis subdenudata
euphorbia suzannae
huernia pillansii

candystore

clothes and sweets for men and women
3153 16th street. between valencia and guerrero
415.863.8143 www.candystore-sf.com
mon - sat noon - 7p sun noon - 6p

opened in 2005. owners: jennifer jones, jenny klowden and marilyn jones
all major credit cards accepted
online shopping. in-store custom alterations

sf : the mission > **s13**

eating candy doesn't seem to go hand in hand with fashion. it's not too hard to imagine super-svelte boutique owners being horrified by the thought of calorie-laden treats passing their lips. the fact that *candystore* offers a big selection of nostalgic candy right next to cute tops and sassy accessories is only one of the reasons this place is a breath of fresh air. with a sweet assortment of labels, this place embodies a carefree, laidback style. and by the way, along with the candy variety, *candystore* has some terrific duds for dudes, too.

covet:
denim:
 wesc
 j brand
 cheap monday
melissa shoes
jackson, johnston & roe
pf flyer
steven alan

church street apothecary

imported sundries and daily basics

1767 church street. corner of 30th
415.970.9828 www.churchapothecary.com
mon - sat 11a - 7p sun 11a - 5p

opened in 2004. owner: kati kim
mc. visa
online shopping

sf : noe valley > **s14**

if *church street apothecary* were in my neighborhood, i would probably look fifteen years younger. which would be one of the many reasons i would often visit this little gem-like shop. during my numerous 'breaks' from writing, i would walk to *c.s.a.* in order to try out the impressive selection of salves, lotions and potions. in addition to loads of these magic potions, they stock other daily necessities like magazines, gum and a large supply of baby needs. basically, this is a neighborhood fountain of youth with sundries.

covet:
mario badescu
ren
malin + goetz
propoline
phyto
pharmacopia
little twig
mason pearson brushes

cookin'

a wonderful selection of top quality, pre-loved cookware

339 divisadero street. between oak and page
415.861.1854
tue - sat noon - 6:30p sun 1 - 5p

opened in 1981. owner: judith kaminsky
visa. mc

sf : nopa > **s15**

in my kitchen, cookware falls into two categories: pretty copper pans from my favorite culinary shop in paris (note: read *eat.shop paris* for details) and enameled cast-iron pieces found at antique and thrift stores. i especially love the latter as the years of loving use by previous owners gives these pans a certain soulfullness. the owner of *cookin'* has employed a similar collecting technique but generously offers these finds for sale. here you will find scads of items that still have plenty of use left in them, and the collection of vintage cookbooks is a culinary history lesson in itself.

covet:
excellent salt & pepper shakers
old french door signs
french r.a.t.p. towels
vintage cookbooks
enamel cast-iron cookware in all shapes & sizes
vintage tin molds
silver creamers

creativity explored

gallery and workshop for artists with developmental disabilities

3245 16th street. between guerrero and dolores
415.863.2108 www.creativityexplored.org
mon - fri 10a - 3p sat 1 - 6p

opened in 1983. founders: dr. elias and florence katz
mc. visa
online shopping. gallery

sf : the mission > **s16**

i look back at sketches i did as a kid and think, "wow, i used to be able to draw!" at some point though, i starting listening to so-called rules, and my drawing skills declined. at *creativity explored*, the non-profit art space for people with developmental disabilities, there are no rules when it comes to art making. these talented people make what they feel, and it's wonderful to see. the most inspiring thing to do is visit the studio while the artists are at work. it conjures the spirit from when creating was free and natural, the way it should be.

covet:
gordon cris donut t's
shadow shine buttons
paper maché airplanes
artist-created notecard sets
jack mckenzie scroll
incredible ceramic sculptures
cross your eyes keep them wide dvd
san francisco icons set

161

cris

designer consignment shop

2056 polk streek. between broadway and pacific
415.474.1191
mon - sat 11a - 6p sun noon - 5p

opened in 1985. owner: cris zander
mc. visa

sf : russian hill > **s17**

in my fantasy world, clothing stores would be more like great bookstores. they would sell super stylish contemporary clothing side by side with incredible vintage pieces, and the prices would be easy on the wallet. good news, friends—there's no need to just fantasize about such a place because there's *cris*. this is a consignment store extraordinaire, where you might find a vintage yves saint laurent piece or a modern-day marni design—*cris* is like a little stroll through recent fashion history.

covet:
marni
marc jacobs
w & l t
moschino
manolo blahnik
louis vuitton
yves saint laurent
chloe

163

doe

tiny department store

629a haight street. between pierce and steiner
415.558.8588 www.doe-sf.com
mon - sat noon - 7p sun noon - 6p

opened in 2004. owner: kati kim
mc. visa
online shopping. gallery

sf lower haight > **s18**

the lower haight is a fun place with many good qualities, but when it comes to shopping it could easily be described as slim pickin's. t.g. for *doe*, which i think of as a tiny department store with a strong point of view that's design conscious, yet lighthearted. despite its eensy size, *doe's* range of offerings is big big big as it carries everything from clothing and housewares to design and apothecary items. i nominate *doe* as lower haight public service citizen of the year.

covet:
deener jeans
thomas paul transferware plates
dutch trade iron-on letters
fluffy co. t's
red flower products
koche backpacks
moss mills jewelry
motaspia dresses

double punch

toys for adults

1821 powell street. corner of filbert
415.399.9785 www.doublepunch.com
mon - sat 11a - 7p sun 11a - 6p

opened in 2004. owner: omar valles and denise wong
all major credit cards accepted
online shopping. gallery

sf : north beach > **s19**

don't tell kaie (the *eat.shop guides* head honcho), but while i am researching these books, i am doing some double-dipping. i've done all of my birthday and christmas shopping for the next few years. between this book and the last one i did for paris, i am stocked up until 2010. at *double punch*, the northbeach store filled with japanese toys for adults with a sense of humor, i bought a great gama go wallet for my niece. for my nephew who loves all things manga, i bought a kaws and pushead figure that he will receive in 2009. it's a sweet deal getting paid to shop.

covet:
tim biskup calli flat pack
pocket stache dolls
takara solar powered flowers
kaws & pushead figures
maffy's marshmallow keychain
minnie mouse mug
gama go wallets
in me own words: the autobiography of bigfoot

167

drift

denim-friendly fashions

815 washington street. between 8th and 9th
510.444.8815 www.driftdenim.com
mon - sat 11a - 7p sun noon - 6p

opened in 2006. owners: alfonso dominguez and johnelle mancha
all major credit cards accepted

east bay : old oakland > s20

if i were a stock-market analyst, and oakland superstar alfonso dominguez's businesses had shares, i would give the thumbs-up for growth potential. he, along with his mother and fiancé, own three businesses in old oakland: stylish *drift*, mouthwatering *tamarindo* (see eat side) and unique *mignonne* which sells home furnishings. this family is single-handedly making old oakland a destination. with *drift*, alfonso has created one of the best places around to find high-end denim and stylish tops. so buy now; this stock of denim is a hot commodity.

covet:
red clay
stronghold
castle
proportion of blu
freedom is natural nirvana
j brand
deener
rag and bone

eden & eden

amazing mix of clothing, housewares and accessories

560 jackson street. corner of columbus avenue
415.983.0490 www.edenandeden.com
mon - fri 10a - 7p sat 10a - 6p sun noon - 6p

opened in 2006. owner: rachel eden
all major credit cards accepted

sf : jackson square > s21

celebrities don't impress me, but people with incredible taste do. i become atwitter, almost star-struck, when i'm in the presence of people with impeccable taste, and i always assume they will judge me. i know this is silly because they never do. at least, rachel didn't when i first visited her store *eden & eden*. this shop mixes new and vintage clothing with housewares and accessories in an effortless way. the clarity of vision here is apparent, yet it is eclectic in the very best of ways. i should learn to not be afraid of the rachels in the world and to be more afraid of the parises and lindsays.

covet:
ivana helsinki handmade clothes
tatty devine facet mirror necklace
established & sons desk lamp
tonfisk finnish ceramics
hand-knit tea cozy
old london bus blinds
donna wilson animals
eden & eden t's

egg & the urban mercantile

modern purveyor of essentials for your home
85 carl street. corner of cole
415.564.2248 www.urbanmercantile.com
tue - sat 11a - 6p sun noon - 5p

opened in 2000. owners: bradley burch and marisa lin
all major credit cards accepted
online shopping. registries. custom orders. home styling

sf : cole valley > s22

egg & the urban mercantile functions like a general store supplying accessory necessities. instead of milk, eggs and sugar, you will find products in these categories: paper, textiles, ceramics, glass, and wood. ok, and sometimes chocolate. items like soft bath towels, fragranced soaps and ceramic vases are chosen for their exceptional qualities and are pleasantly displayed for you to browse. so instead of having your honey pick up a dozen eggs on the way home, i suggest having him/her pick up some lina felicia pillows instead.

covet:
potluck studios textiles
david fussenegger textiles
bubble roome soaps & lotions
whitney smith ceramics
chocolate bar new york chocolates
paper*ink studio cards
celia designs ceramics
twill terry towels

erica tanov

stylish, sophisticated fashions from a california native

2408 fillmore street. between washington and jackson. 415.674.1228
berkeley: 1827 fourth street. between virginia and hearst. 510.849.3331
www.ericatanov.com
mon - sat 11a - 6p sun 11a - 5p

opened in 2005. owner: erica tanov
all major credit cards accepted

sf : pacific heights / east bay : berkeley > s23

i have no idea if ms. tanov would like me, but i sure like her. my crush started the minute i walked into her new-ish shop on fillmore street. all the details were perfect—erica's designs are clean and subtle with a quiet gracefulness. items are made with fine fabrics and meticulous constructions that express feminin- ity and self confidence. since opening her first bou- tique in berkeley, her line has expanded beyond women's clothing to bed linens and children's cloth- ing. erica, you have a large and devoted following of which i am now a card-carrying member.

covet:
erica tanov everything
beaded scarves
dorotea shoes
melissa joy manning jewelry
pippa small jewelry
virginia johnson clothing
pare umbrellas
klife enamel

fantastico

if you're going to open a party shop, make sure to give it a zinger of a name. i recommend calling it *hypersensational extraordinarilicious awesomeocity*. if not that, then *fantastico* is the next best name. this place is a wonderland of unbelievable goods for parties, crafts and holiday decorating. located in a huge warehouse south of market, this place has any silk flower, tissue-paper ball or christmas ornament ever desired. are you throwing a bar mitzvah and your colors are sky and puce? *fantastico* has what you need. yes sirree, this place is fabulous-ful.

covet:
piñatas
candles in every color
plastic tiki masks
paper party sculptures
party plates
disco balls in every size
tiaras
balloons

177

fiddlesticks

stylish clothes for two to eight year olds

508 hayes street. between octavia and laguna
415.565.0508 www.shopfiddlesticks.com
mon - sat 11a - 7p sun 11a - 6p

opened in 2007. owner: elizabeth leu
all major credit cards accepted

sf : hayes valley > s25

i guarantee there was no *fiddlesticks* around when i was a kid, at least not in rural illinois, and i have the class pictures to prove it. as kids we did not have cool stores like *fiddlesticks*, or the cool clothing they carry. instead we had strange winnie the pooh stuff that came in colors that were reminiscent of the disliked crayon colors from the crayola box. kids, if you're reading this, you are lucky. you are not going to need years of therapy getting over your class pictures. thanks to *fiddlesticks* you will grow up to be well adjusted, stylish adults. lucky little buggers.

covet:
neige
glug baby
wonderboy
okkies for boys
tea collection
camper for kids
scoop
see kai run

179

flora grubb gardens

nursery of exotic plants and good things for the garden

1634 jerrold avenue. between 3rd and phelps
415.648.2670 www.floragrubb.com
mon - sat 8a - 6p sun 10a - 6p

opened in 2007. owner: flora grubb
all major credit cards accepted
classes. design services

at the recently transplanted *flora grubb gardens,* the fine selection of plants is only part of the story. yes, you will find the best offering of perennials anywhere in the city. and the selection of full-grown palm trees can only be described as paradise worthy. such a collection of garden accouterment makes the hike to bay view seem like a necessity. a chinese chippendale garden set could be the pièce de résistance for my "golden girls" fantasy lanai. and i must admit, the collection of japanese pruners made me want to tear out my entire yard and go bonsai.

covet:
aloe plicatilis
aeonium canariense
perch birdfeeder
guerrero street yellow metal watering can
japanese handmade pruners
spear & jackson shovels
west county gloves
chinese chippendale garden furniture set

gamescape

333 divisadero street. between oak and page
415.621.4263
mon - sat 10a - 7p sun 11a - 5p

opened in 1985. owner: robert hamilton
all major credit cards accepted
game events.   self-serve gift wrapping

along with my annual resolution to eat and drink more, my new year's pledge this year was to play more games. no kidding. in fact, my friend storm and i try to play d & d every day. we make excuses like "it keeps our aging minds sharp." i figure games like d & d help me plot strategic, tactical plans to become ruler of the *eat.shop* empire. this is one reason i love *gamescape* as their selection of chess and backgammon boards is unsurpassed. and they stock almost every new and nostalgic game known to man, including twister. balancing exercises, anyone?

covet:
classic board games:
  scrabble
  clue
  mousetrap
deluxe backgammon sets
lightweight roll-up chess sets
dominos of all shapes & sizes
dart supplies

183

goorin hat shop

local hat makers since 1895

1612 stockton street. corner of union
415.402.0454 www.goorin.com
mon - fri 11a - 7p sat 10a - 8p sun 11a - 4p

opened in 2006. owner: ben goorin
all major credit cards accepted
online shopping

sf : north beach > **s28**

ben goorin opened this little den of dapperness last year. like a wood-paneled library complete with rolling ladders, *goorin hat shop* harkens back to the day when men would don stylish noggin' attire. as you might guess from his last name, ben knows a bit about hat-making. he is the current descendant of the goorin hat family who have been making caps for s.f. craniums since 1895. you can find everything here from modern lids to classicly inspired fur felt hats complete with vintage tie silk bands. think rat pack when donning one, but wear it with local pride.

covet:
hats:
  thorns (cadet)
  embroidered baseball
  classic fur felt with vintage tie silk
  rodge
  knit beanies
four square clutch
the muffin mayford bag

harputs market

the harputs have been making people look cool for a long time. the family owns the legendary tennis shoe shop where many a rock star has purchased enviable vintage footwear. now the harput's bring a bit o' glamour next door, to their beautifully designed shop *harputs market*. here is where you can find sought after, cutting-edge designers' wares rarely seen in the bay area. hussein chalayan dresses and junya watanabe pieces are as covetable as it gets in the world of high fashion. so keep your eyes out for the rock stars; they're certain to be lurking around here.

covet:
y's by yohji yamamoto
umbro by kim jones
the breed
hussein chalayan
sara lanzi
junya watanabe
maison martin margiela
dead stock vintage eyewear

herringbone

1527 shattuck avenue. between vine and cedar
510.649.9442 www.herringboneshop.com
tue - sat 11a - 6p sun noon - 5p

opened in 2005. owner: shawn burke
mc. visa
spa services

east bay : berkeley : gourmet ghetto > s30

close your eyes. imagine you're in a rustic mountain cabin. the walls are paneled with knotty pine and dotted with interesting contemporary art… huh? be patient, dreamers, and stick with me. throughout this cabin are deliciously sought-after beauty products and luxury items displayed on unpolished wooden shelves. the image i depict is *herringbone*, a modern apothecary and spa. here you'll find a groovy selection of hard-to-find items in an environment much more berkshires than bergdorfs. this is like a glamorous retreat tucked in the hinterlands.

covet:
herringbone handmade makeup brushes
aftelier perfume
proraso shaving creme
lipstick queen
burn candles
skyn products from iceland
sara lapp lip scrubs
titus makeup bags

189

hida tool

beloved japanese tool store

1333 san pablo avenue. corner of gilman
510.524.3700 www.hidatool.com
mon - sat 9a - 6p

opened in 1986. owner: osamu hiroyama
all major credit cards accepted
tool sharpening and repair

east bay : berkeley > s31

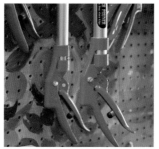

"toy stores for adults," that's what some people call boat or electronics stores. mind you, that's some people, not me—i'll never have a "he who dies with the most toys wins" bumper sticker. but *hida tool*, the adored japanese tool store, now that's my kind of toy store. everything is fascinating and desirable. tiny metal clippers made for cutting string, multi-colored gardening twine, and a bamboo winnow so well made it looks as if a woman could wear it on her head to a paris fashion show. everything is so beautiful, you'll be tempted to keep your purchases under hurricane glass.

covet:
copper rain chains
bamboo splitters
japanese wooden planes
bonsai tools
bamboo winnow
shoji brushes
string cutters
twines

191

house of hengst

stylishly understated clothing boutique for men and women

924 valencia. between 20th and 21st
415.642.0841 www.houseofhengst.com
mon - fri noon - 7p sat 11a - 7p sun 11a - 6p

opened in 2001. owner: susan hengst
all major credit cards accepted
online shopping. gallery

sf : the mission > s32

my personal style falls on the side of simple. i reserve my showy self for verbal outbursts and outrageous expressions in eating. but on the occasions when i want to pump my look up a bit, i head to *house of hengst*. these stylish clothes with utterly perfect detailing allow me to feel pulled together without being too peacocky. and i must admit, i'm a bit jealous, as women have a fantastic selection to choose from here. the "dream" dress is made from pale blush silk jersey that could put the slink back in your slinky.

covet:
hengst:
  "garcia" coat
  silk jersey "dream" dress
  stripe viscose rib "bonnie" dress
  pink linen "veranda" pant
adoura demode jewelry
the fit hats by alison
turk & taylor shirts

193

in fiore

couture body balms and oils

868 post street. between hyde and leavenworth
415.928.5661 www.infiore.net
tue - fri noon - 6p sat 10a - 6p

opened in 2006. owner: julie elliott
all major credit cards accepted
online shopping

sf : the tenderloin > s33

how smart is julie? the owner of *in fiore* has come up with the most ingenious way to experience her scents. rather than the typical spraying your arm and flapping like a bird in order to sniff each scent, julie has put together a collection of blank books infused with her signature scents. you simply choose by label, leaf through the book, and the action supplies a gentle hint of the scent. this ingenuity should come as no surprise. since founding her brand, she has been supplying the discerning with her holistic skincare to rave reviews. bloomin' wonderful.

covet:
in fiore products
dayna decker candles
amajio toothpaste
historic fragrance lamps
liebling deodorant
haute concentrates
international orange products
jimmy jane candles

kamei restaurant supply

525 - 547 clement street. between 6th and 7th
415.666.3688
mon - sun 9a - 7p

opened in 1993. owners: ms. wong
mc. visa

sf : inner richmond > **s34**

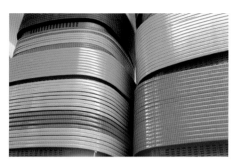

if you're a cook, you will love *kamei restaurant supply*. if you're looking for a gift for a hard-to-buy-for friend, you will love *kamei restaurant supply*. if you are just curious about other cultures, good for you, you should be. *kamei* is one of those rare finds—a virtual galaxy of all things asian, it makes me want skip up and down the aisles collecting gizmos as i go. it's an enormous place and stocks everything from woks and rice paper lanterns to orchids and graters for foods i didn't even realize your could grate. *kamei* is the best deal in town.

covet:
meat cleavers
ginger graters
paper lanterns
woks & wok accouterments
dehydrated towels
tea pots & strainers
zojurishi rice makers
orchids

mac (modern appealing clothing)

must-visit men's and women's fashion boutique

387 grove street. between gough and franklin
415.863.3011
mon - sat 11a - 7p sun noon - 6p

opened in 1980. owners: chris ospital and ben ospital
all major credit cards accepted

sf : hayes valley > **s35**

if you are one who knows your way around a big city and a thing or two about fashion, you have no doubt heard of *mac*. you've heard of it because this brother and sister team have gathered one of the preeminent collections of high-end fashion in the bay area. the fact that they are sweet as pie, without a hint of that look-down-your-nose-you're-not-skinny-enough-to-wear-this-stuff attitude certainly doesn't hurt business either. if you don't already know about *mac*, fold down the corner of this page—no doubt you're going to want to swing in and find something amazing.

covet:
ting
dries van noten
dirk van saene
tsumori chisato
zero
dema
engineered garments
lisa jenks jewelry

magnet

stylish clothing for women

2508 san pablo. corner of dwight
510.848.1966 www.magnetboutique.com
tue - sat 11a - 6p sun noon - 5p

opened in 2005. owner: camille mason
all major credit cards accepted

east bay : west berkeley > **s36**

after walking around looking at clothes and design for awhile, you begin to feel a bit hypnotized by seeing the hot trend or the hot designer over and over again. so when i walked into *magnet*, the first thing i said to myself was "wow, someone here has a great eye and is an individualist." the comely camille has gathered together a spectacular mix of regional and up-and-coming national designers. the look here is sophisticated silhouettes with a stylish and young verve. i am hypnotized by *magnet*.

covet:
black label
talla
del forte
corey lynn calter
lewis cho
tinc
billy blues
bone dust jewelry

minnie wilde

spunky women's clothing

3266 21st street. between valencia and mission
415.642.9453 www.minniewilde.com
mon - fri noon - 7p sat 11a - 7p sun 11a - 5p

opened in 2001. owners: terri olson and ann d'apice
mc. visa
online shopping. registries. gallery

a lot of people are stylish—they can put outfits together that look good. other people transcend style and have a sort of magical, mysterious secret sense about mixing clothing with such fanciful and imaginative combinations that it becomes something sensational. *minnie wilde's* eponymous line mixed with some of the other designers represented here can help you be one of those style transcenders. take note though: this is not the place for work clothes at *h&r block*. but if you have some fashion spunk, and a dash of kick ass, *minnie wilde* is the ticket.

covet:
minnie wilde clothing
spring & clifton
jordache
wowch
sonja benevides jewelry
bergamot brass works
dean bags
dv shoes

mixed use

vintage furnishings and fashion

463 union street. between grant and kearny
415.956.1909 www.mixedusemodern.com
mon - sun 11a - 7p sun noon - 6p

opened in 2005. owner: katherine johnstone
mc. visa

sf : north beach > **s38**

when this guide becomes one of oprah's picks and i become obscenely rich (stop snickering, it could happen)... i will use my earnings to fund a movie about my life. it will be about a child of the '70s who wants to break out of his shell and take on the world. i don't know who will play me yet, but i do know that i will send my set designers to *mixed use* to find just the right decor and fashions to style my biopic. here they'll find the reel-to-reel tape deck and lucite bookends to prop the scene where i put pencil to paper. this movie will be titled "get over yourself, jon."

covet:
cool, old eight-track player
lucite & chrome lamps
empire troubador turntable
style-y vintage men's suits
vintage bose speaker stack
cool bent plywood shelving unit
iittala festivo candle holders
marimekko fabrics

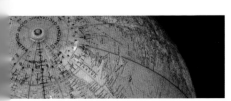

mollusk surf shop

surf shop and art gallery
4500 irving street. corner of 46th
415.564.6300 www.mollusksurfshop.com
mon - sun 10a - 6:30p

opened in 2005. owner: john mccambridge
mc. visa
online shopping. custom orders. gallery

sf : outer sunset > s39

i have never been on a surfboard. i grew up in illinois where surfing is not part of the curriculum. drive a combine, yes—hang ten, no. growing up a thousand miles from the nearest ocean, my experience with killer waves came mostly through the clothing. functioning as a full-service surf shop and art gallery, *mollusk* seems to fit into my current life. i can still dream of riding a long board while buying surf britches and at the same time checking out the artwork of young, local artists. *mollusk* also commissions artists to print cool t's which will surely finish off my surfer look.

covet:
handmade surfboards
artist commissioned t's
birdwell shorts
rainbow hemp flip-flops
custom board bags
surf maps
hero underwater camera
sprout dvd

monument

high-end, vintage "modern" design

572 valencia street. between 16th and 17th
415.861.9800 www.monument.1stdibs.com
mon - thu noon - 6p fri - sat noon - 7p sun noon - 6p

opened in 2005. owners: michael de angelis and samuel genthner
all major credit cards accepted
online shopping

sf : the mission > **s40**

everyone used to have a story of finding some incredible piece of modern design for next to nothing at an estate sale. but, honestly, when is the last time someone found such a deal? the days of finding a knoll sectional for $5 are over. unless you are some sort of secret superhero who is able to sniff out mid-century treasures, you're gonna have to pay retail. *monument* is the destination for finding a flawless piece to accent your home. the owners here should be named "the aalto avenger" and "captain saarinen" befitting their supernatural talents at finding the good stuff.

covet:
limberg chandelier
vladimir kagan chair
furnette walnut buffet
lucite sculptures
holmegaard glass
hans belling birds
asian ceramic pendant light
florence knoll sectional

my trick pony

custom printing and artist-designed clothing

742 14th street. between belcher and market
415.861.0595 www.mytrickpony.com
tue - sat 11:30a - 7p sun noon - 5p

opened in 2005. owner: matteo tacchini
mc. visa
custom design. gallery

sf : the castro > **s41**

i hate the phrase "you look like you're having too much fun." it sounds like something a sour-faced fussbudget would say. you'll find no f.b.'s at *my trick pony*. this place is so fun it would be fine if they didn't sell anything. you would still visit for the carnival-like atmosphere with pony figurines and colorful maquettes decorating the space. other than a store, this is a graphic design studio that sells their (and other artists') designs on shirts, bags, undies or whatever. as if there wasn't enough merriment, they throw movie events complete with printed t's as party favors. whoopee!

covet:
chrome bags
screen-printed undies
trucker hats
artist-designed & printed t's
airbrush designs
printed ties
custom graphics
fuzzy transfer letters

211

nest

ethnic-inspired mix of housewares and clothing

2300 fillmore street. corner of clay
415.292.6199
mon - sat 10:30a - 6:30p sun 11:30 - 6p

opened in 1995. owners: judy gilman and marcella madsen
all major credit cards accepted
registries

sf : pacific heights > **s42**

how i would love to be a bird. to be able to spend my days flapping about freely, watching the world go by. it fills me with yearning. a bird gets to migrate to sunny climes for the winter and make its home in whatever tree it fancies. well, at least in this lifetime i won't be a bird, but i can still collect special things to pad my nest and make it cozy. at the aptly named *nest*, there are loads of worthy materials to spruce up your world. covetable items like better living pillows and jolom mayaetik textiles make this terrestrial life more sensuous and colorful.

covet:
better living pillows
cydwoq sandals
barbara schriber designs
chan luu clothes
pooki & co dolls
jolom mayaetik textiles
riedizioni purses
moro: the cookbook

213

nida

544 hayes street. between octavia and laguna
415.552.4670
mon - sat 11a - 7p sun noon - 6p

opened in 2001. owner: kiko giobbio
all major credit cards accepted

sf : hayes valley > **s43**

most of the time, i don't want to get noticed when i go into a fancy clothing boutique. i never expect the first question out of the shop person's mouth to be "can i help you?" but rather, "sorry, no jon harts allowed." sometimes my unreasonable fear keeps me outside looking in. but at *nida*, the welcome mat is out. though they have all of the ammunition to lay it on thick here from raf simmons to cacheral, they choose bonhomie. not only is the staff super helpful, but the pleasant space is just the right size to take a peak at something special without getting daunted by endless choices.

covet:
neil barret
raf simmons
junya watanabe
vanessa bruno
isabel marant
paul & joe
rogan
y3

nisa san francisco

cool clothes and accessories for the ladies

3789 24th street. between church and dolores
3610 19th street. corner of guerrero
415.920.9149 www.nisasf.com
mon - sat 11a - 7p sun noon - 6p

opened in 2006. owners: shinobu sering, umay mohammed,
ivy chan & marie biscarra
all major credit cards accepted

sf : noe valley / the mission > s44

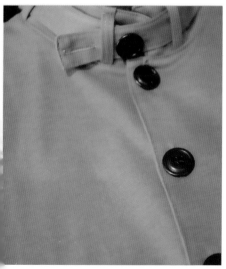

it takes a girl with a strong sense of self to bring back fashion moments like "princess di hair." eventually the world rotates backwards and nothing looks fresher than a short, feathered, blown-out bob. it's this type of thinking that drives the creative minds behind *nisa*, a s.f.-based clothing design company. here you will find cool clothes for girls with a need to express their inner style. ski vests with ruffled mary ingalls wilder sleeves and geometric shirt dresses that have more than just a whiff of "flashdance." *nisa* ladies, i'll be on the lookout for "9 to 5" chic soon.

covet:
nisa designs:
   knickerbocker pant
   triple threat dress
   frilly vest
   inca dress
   phoenix dress
kris nation rings
hand-woven brazilian earrings

park life

museum store without admission

220 clement street. between 3rd and 4th
415.386.7275 www.parklifestore.com
sun - thu noon - 8p fri - sat noon - 9p

opened in 2006. owners: jamie alexander and derek song
all major credit cards accepted
online shopping. gallery

sf : inner richmond > **s45**

let's just get this straight: i'm not one of those people who goes to a museum just to go to the shop. i like to look at the artwork… 'cause it puts me in the mood to buy things when i'm done. *park life* knows this secret formula and has shrunken it to a smaller scale. in the back of their space they have rotating shows of inspiring artwork. in the front, there's a selection of extremely well-curated objects, books, and t's—all appealing to those with artistic sensibilities. and soon *park life* will publish art books under their own imprint. so it seems they are an institution in the making.

covet:
david shrigley limited-edition housewares
qubus glassware
wooden toy catapult
fluffy company t's
t. p. l. lighters
eggling plant kits
mmckenna led light kits
peggy honeywell green mountain cd

paxton gate

bones, plants, tea, minerals, taxidermy and good times

824 valencia street. between 19th and 20th
415.824.1872 www.paxtongate.com
mon - fri noon - 7p sat - sun 11a - 7p

opened in 1992. owner: sean quigley
all major credit cards accepted
online shopping. registries. classes. landscape & design. custom orders

sf : the mission > **s46**

if the taxidermy curator from the museum of natural history circa early 20th century teamed up with tim burton and opened an antique and plant store, it would look a lot like *paxton gate*. this strangely enticing store is a must-see for people whose tastes are a bit off-beat. look for a large selection of carnivorous plants along with fascinating taxidermied animals, some dressed in victorian regalia. the selection of nursery equipment is top notch and intermingled with interesting tea supplies. *paxton* gate is the most enjoyable entertainment since johnny depp learned to trim hedges.

covet:
monique motyl skull dolls
lisa kinoshita jewelry
staghorn ferns
native carnivorous plants
nature's best hummingbird feeders
jeanie m taxidermy mice
tillandsia (air plants)
integral teapot with cup

peace industry

traditional and contemporary iranian felt rugs

535 octavia. corner of ivy
415.255.9940 www.peaceindustry.com
mon - fri 10a - 6p sat 11a - 6p sun 11a - 5p

opened in 2005. owners: melina and dodd raissnia
all major credit cards accepted
custom orders. occasional classes. gift wrapping

sf : hayes valley > **s47**

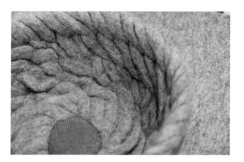

when i realized that the rugs on display at *peace industry* were actually huge pieces of felt, i thought "wow, why hasn't anyone thought of this before?" then i watched a video of the manufacturing process and realized my wow idea was a thousand years late. this method of rug making is actually an ancient iranian art that the owners of *peace industry* are helping to keep alive. using iranian manufacturers, melina takes this ancient art form and modernizes it with her colorful geometric designs. i will never look at a felt rug the same way again.

covet:
melina raissnia design felt rugs:
  big flower
  box
  field
  round & ovals
kevin harris pillows
emily nachison felt baskets
turkoman robes

propeller

contemporary home-design store
555 hayes street. between laguna and octavia
415.701.7767 www.propellermodern.com
mon - sat 11a - 7p sun noon - 5p

opened in 2003. owner: lorn dittfeld
all major credit cards accepted
custom orders

sf : hayes valley > s48

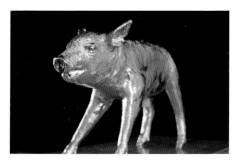

as one of the most forward home-design stores in s.f., *propeller* should be treated as a public service. the examples of design available here gently educate people about what is happening in the world of contemporary design. they in no way dictate what color couch you should have this year; rather, *propeller* functions as a resource on perspective. tables by harry allen, chris kabels parasol and many other fine examples provide a venue to understand this ever-changing world. rather than getting stuck in the middle of last century, *propeller* securely moves us into the next.

covet:
niels bendtsen drop in sectional
ron gilad fruit bowl & void table
hakusan porcelain
established & sons lamps
sara paloma vases
droog bottoms up doorbell
saikai ceramics
tord boontje rug

rose and radish

inspiring home decor and flowers

460 gough street. between hayes and grove
415.864.4988 www.roseandradish.com
tue - sat 10a - 6p

opened in 2006. owner: cate kellison
all major credit cards accepted
online shopping. registries

formerly a high-end flower shop, *rose and radish* has become a haven for highly curated and scarcely available home-design objects. you can still buy perfect perennials at this pristine space, but now they are intermixed with items ranging from dishware to wallpaper. these objects, which are sourced from around the world, are displayed art gallery style—meaning every couple of months there's a new show with fresh products. this inspiring approach to home decor is taken even further by cate, who also commissions local artists to create art specifically for the space. awesome.

covet:
inv/alt design snap cups
atypyk gun ruler
industreal chapeaux pour vase
industreal 72 dpi lamp
anne kyyro quin block cushion cover
christian tortu golf vase
zack wide & high watering can
la corbeille sugar handle set

227

salon des parfums

exclusive purveyor of henry jacques parfums

210 post street, suite 511. corner of grant
415.982.1500 www.salondesparfums.com
tue - sat noon - 6p

opened in 2002. owner: kevin hoskins
all major credit cards accepted
personal service

sf : union square > **s50**

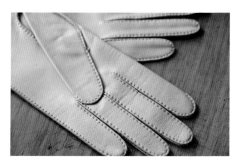

i thought i was fancy because i own a fragrance from a place in london that holds a warrant of appointment to the queen. well, i had no idea that truly fancy people have someone help pick their scents specifically for them. at *salon des parfums*, the exclusive french line of henry jacques scents are represented. in this intimate setting, you sample and sniff until you find just the right notes of scent that suit you. this level of personal attention feels good, and the range and quality of parfums is amazing. i couldn't place the origins of the scent "deep oudh," but i knew it was the one for me.

covet:
henry jacques parfums:
 salvatore
 jasmin absolut
 deep oudh
 etoile
 lilas bebe
 attar anu'ud
daniel storto handmade italian leather gloves

self edge

exclusive purveyor of hard-to-find japanese denim

714 valencia street. corner of 18th
415.558.0658 www.selfedge.com
mon - sat noon - 7p sun noon - 5p

opened in 2006. owner: kiya babzani and demitra georgopoulos
all major credit cards accepted
online shopping. custom alterations

sf : the mission > **s51**

selvedge is the holy grail for denim afficionados. the term refers to the edge of woven fabrics, sometimes un-dyed, that comes from denim produced on old-style, high-quality looms. you will find this subtle detail only on denim of the highest caliber. a play on the word, *self edge* is more than a jeans shop, it's a store for collectors who seek out denim of this quality. kiya has gone to exhaustive lengths to gather the greatest selection of denim from around the world. this unwavering eye for detail continues into the exceptional tops and accessories. this is as good as it gets.

covet:
denim:
  flat head (only u.s. distribution)
  iron heart (only u.s. distribution)
  skull jeans by an alchemist
  quality clothing
  sugarcane
  samurai jeans
  mama

slash

vintage levi's jeans and cords

2840 college avenue. corner of russell
510.841.7803 www.slashberkeley.com
mon - sat 11a - 7p sun noon - 5p

opened in 1979. owners: carla bell and chris grace
all major credit cards accepted

east bay : berkeley : elmwood > s52

after finishing my *eat.shop* research, i told friends about what i had found in my travels. when i showed pics of the teetering stacks of vintage jeans and cords at *slash*, i had a friend beg me not to publish the address until he could get there and skim off the top. i said that i had taken a hippocratic oath, but not to worry, there was plenty, as *slash* is a treasure trove. if you're looking for a specific model or color of vintage levi's, talk to carla, and she dives in and magically finds the wished-for pants. if vintage is not your thing, *slash* just opened a shop of more modern styles upstairs.

covet:
robert miller shirts & striped scarves
surplus russian long underwear
oodles of vintage levi's cords
yak pak bags
vintage denim in all shapes & sizes
vintage western shirts
military jackets

stem

flowers and things for the home

3690 18th street. between dolores and guerrero
415.861.7836 www.stemsf.com
mon - thu 11a - 6:30p fri 11a - 6p sat - sun 10:30a - 5:30p

opened in 2005. owners: maxine siu and joel bleskacek
all major credit cards accepted
delivery. weddings

sf : the mission > s53

while volunteering with the forest service, i learned that when a forest is healthy and in balance, only then will there be a sustainable mix of plants and flowers working in unison within the forest community. it may sound strange, but i see the mission neighborhood as a healthy, flourishing forest. and the flower/object shop *stem* is like the forest trillium that sprouts when conditions are perfect. *stem* is an integral part of the area by supplying beautiful flowers, comfortable and covetable objects to it's neighbors. a wonderful cooperation.

covet:
lilacs & rununculas
barefoot dream robes
little twig shirts
dani candles
etched parisian glassware
pinecone & chickadee screen printed cards
baby star bibs
glug baby clothes

supple

skincare services & beauty products

1543 hopkins street. between sacramento and monterey
510.525.7068 www.suppleintegrative.com
tue - thu 11a - 6p fri - sat 10a - 6p

opened in 2004. owner: alison supple evans
mc. visa
spa services

east bay : berkeley : monterey market > **s54**

at *supple* the mood is peaceful. alison has done a great job at creating an environment free from everyday anxieties. this is a place to beautify after all, so one should not feel anxious trying to decide between an antioxidant infusion or the supple bespoke treatment. however, i can't guarantee your heart won't be a-pumpin' by the hard-to-find product lines. when you realize you have discovered a source for lines like arcona, you might start to panic and think, "i should buy them all." take a breath, make an appointment for a holistic purification, and know that *supple* is here for you.

covet:
products:
  ren
  cowshed
  this works
  in fiore
  arcona
  kimberly sayer
  astara

tail of the yak

an institution of creativity

2632 ashby avenue. between college and benvenue
510.841.9891
mon - sat 11a - 5:30p

opened in 1972. owners: alice hoffman erb and lauren swan mcintosh
all major credit cards accepted
registries. custom printing

east bay : berkeley : elmwood > **s55**

making a pilgrimage to the *tail of the yak* is on many people's agendas as this is a bay area institution. here, everything seems to be just a bit magical. balls of twine are somehow elevated to precious and extraordinary artifacts, and rare and treasured items are given their due diligence. this level of appreciation does not happen by accident but has everything to do with the two creative women who opened this shop more than thirty years ago. they have nurtured creativity and beauty here, and that's a treasure for us all to explore.

covet:
radiometers from germany
surprise balls
antique georgian jewelry
cast gun metal bird feet
imported twines
letterpress cards by julie holcomb
antique maps
surprise shells

the ribbonerie

rare and hard-to-find ribbons, trims, laces and embellishments

3695 sacramento street. corner of spruce
415.626.6184 www.theribbonerie.com
tue - fri 11a - 6p sat 11a - 5p

opened in 1997. owner: paulette knight
all major credit cards accepted
custom orders. occasional classes. gift wrapping

sf : laurel heights > s56

do you need to festoon a present or an article of clothing with a ribbon adornment? i often do. and when in s.f., i do it at *the ribbonerie*. paulette travels to paris to stock the best selection of new and antique ribbons this side of, well… france. in fact, her stock of french wired ribbons, the really pretty stuff that can be bent to hold a shape is unsurpassed. giving a gift wrapped with a piece of screen printed grosgrain from *the ribbonerie* will make anybody happy. unless, of course, you give them the "desperate housewives" boardgame.

covet:
french wired ribbon
french grosgrain
passe menterie
antique ric rac
antique jacquard ribbons
vintage laces
soutache
brocades

241

the seventh heart

affordable fashion

1592 market street. corner of page
415.431.1755 myspace.com/theseventhheart
mon - fri 11a - 7p sat 11a - 6p

opened in 2005. owners: jess cuevas and mark hoke
mc. visa

sf : deco ghetto / hayes valley > **s57**

unless you're a hollywood starlet and you get to go shopping for fabulous clothing for fabulous events— most of the time, most of us mere mortals buy clothing for everyday. enter *the seventh heart*, whose mission is to provide affordable fashion to the groovy folk. there is a hipster focus here, especially in the exceptional selection of jeans, which tend to be on the slimmy side. whether that will fit your hip(s)ness level or not, you will surely find a cool accessory or cute little summer t-shirt to keep you going until you become a supersta.

covet:
cheap monday jeans
option-g t's
"alternative" hats
alex & chloe jewelry
no star t's
heavy rotation clothing
loads of levi's
horseface hankies

the wok shop

718 grant avenue. between clay and commercial
415.989.3797 www.wokshop.com
mon - sun 10a - 6p

opened in 1970. owner: tane chan
all major credit cards accepted
online shopping. custom orders

sf : chinatown > s58

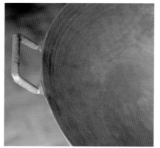

this is how i research these books. i gather scads of recommendations, i scour magazines and newspapers, i search the internet, and most importantly i spend many, many hours on foot searching the city for gems. then i gather all my notes from this research and dive in. the day i began work on this book, i started near the end of my list with *the wok shop*. it went to the top of my favorites quickly. there was every type of asian cooking utensil i have envied for years—so i purchased a new cast-iron wok, a brush, a cleaver and a cool cutting board. i like this job.

covet:
fabulous hand-hammered pow wok
traditional cast-iron wok
super mac knives
wok cleaning brushes
cast iron tea pots
japanese lacquer spoons
bamboo utensils
extensive cleaver selection

245

tsurukichi indigo

gorgeous japanese indigo

864 post street. between hyde and leavenworth
415.292.5550 www.indigojapan.com
tue - sat 11a - 6p or by appointment

opened in 2006. owner: matt dick
all major credit cards accepted
custom orders

sf : tenderloin > s59

traditional indigo fabric has to be seen firsthand in order to appreciate its intricate subtleties, and *tsurukichi* is the place to see it. matt has teamed up with a centuries-old japanese indigo factory and makes clothing from their rich and vibrant fabrics. his knowledge of fashion and japanese history are apparent through the exquisite details and the ultra-chic designs. showing me a fabric covered with tiny polka dots, he explained that a tiny pucker of fabric was tied every half-inch and then the whole thing dyed. wow, this is not the same process you did at home in 1974.

covet:
natural cotton indigo-dyed t's
custom-made aprons
indigo jeans
custom dyeing
totes
multi turbine
custom-designed kimonos
indigo yardage

twenty two shoes

with the wagonloads of shoes available out there, isn't it amazing how hard it is to find something great? some people buy everything and anything in hopes something beautiful will rise to the top; others have a couple of old standbys that they wear to tatters. never fear, *twenty two shoes* can solve all your shoe woes. they not only have their own stylish, yet incredibly wearable designs that are made in italy but other great lines as well. so stop the great shoe search and get your feet a-walkin' here.

covet:
house line:
  the atia
  the leo
  the charlie
  the nubia
lolas lolos lolitos
loeffler randall
sequoia bags

249

x21

modern vintage housewares and oddities

890 valencia street. corner of 20th
415.647.4211 www.x21modern.com
mon - thu noon - 6p fri - sun noon - 7p

opened in 1996. owners: john conaty and dave shaw
mc. visa
online shopping

sf : the mission > **s61**

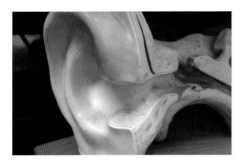

there is something wonderful about shopping at *x21*. it exists somewhere between a museum of oddities and a really great vintage furniture store. the only question is whether anybody really uses this stuff, but that's not the point. the real point is, if i woke up this morning and decided to decorate my house like a high school theater production of cleopatra but set it in the future or on the moon, i would know exactly where to go shopping. besides the truly outrageous examples of home decor, there are loads of incredibly tasteful items also—but you know you want the king tut statue.

covet:
absolutely giant swatch wall clock
elephant footstool
giant head parade costumes
egyptian king tut statue
grade-school wall maps
antique medical equipment
giant mounted swordfish
bronze palm tree table

yone of san francisco

unique bead and adornment shop

478 union street. between grant and varennes
415.986.1424 www.yonebee.com
mon - tue noon - 5p thu - sat noon - 5p

opened in 1969. owner: mr. bee
all major credit cards accepted

back in the summer of love, a bead store called *yone* opened in s.f. over the years, it's become a renowned resource for beautiful, unusual, and unique adornments. lining the walls, the stacks of tiny boxes marked with handwritten numbers document the history and the growth of this store. today, as new generations of creative types come to this gem looking for something special, we are in the summer of the surge—love has taken a back seat. thankfully though, mr. bee continues sharing his wisdom with anyone in the market for a beautiful bead.

covet:
beads:
  glass
  semi-precious
  stone
  amber
  wood
  bone
jewelry-making equipment

zoë bikini

custom and handmade bikinis
3386 18th street. corner of mission
415.621.4551 www.zoebikini.com
mon - sat noon - 7p

opened in 2007. owner: zoë magee
mc. visa
custom orders. bikini parties

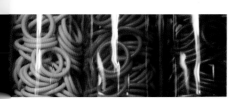

surely it is no surprise that *zoë bikini* sells bikinis. but what might be a surprise is that zoë makes them all herself, in her shop just off of mission street. even more amazing is one can have a bikini made specifically to fit your… um… needs. there are three categories of custom bikinis. #1—the original: it's all about fitting your special curves. #2—made just for you: it's truly bespoke, made with any fabric or hardware you can find. #3—the knockoff: a remake of that incredible-fitting string number you found on the riviera. and there's ready-to-wear, too. what more could you ask for?

covet:
custom-made zoë suits:
  the original
  made just for you
  the knock-off
  addition
ready-to-wear bikinis
beach & sun needs

notes

etc.

the eat.shop guides were created by kaie wellman and are published by cabazon books.

eat.shop sf bay area second edition was written, researched and photographed by jon hart.

editing: kaie wellman   copy editing: lynn king   fact checking: emily withrow
additional production: julia dickey

jon thx: nicole and todd, colleen and avram, patrick, rachel, kaie, and all of the businesses featured in this book.

cabazon books: eat.shop sf east bay second edition
ISBN-13 978-0-9789588-4-8

the eat.shop guides are distributed by independent publishers group: www.ipgbook.com

to find more about the eat.shop guides: www.eatshopguides.com

PRINTED IN SINGAPORE